GOOD FOOD FAST

GOOD FOOD FAST

Emily Jonzen

 National Trust

For the happiest, bravest boy
and chief taste tester, Albie

First published in the United Kingdom in 2022 by
National Trust Books
43 Great Ormond Street
London WC1N 3HZ

Copyright © National Trust Books, 2022
Text © Emily Jonzen
The moral rights of the author have been asserted.

ISBN 9781911657415

A CIP catalogue record for this book is available from the
British Library.

30 29 28 27 26 25 24 23 22
10 9 8 7 6 5 4 3 2 1

Reproduction by Rival Colour Ltd, UK
Printed and bound by Toppan Leefung Ltd, China

This book is available at National Trust shops and online at
www.nationaltrustbooks.co.uk

Introduction

With seemingly never-ending demands on our time, thinking about what to cook and eat can very easily fall down our list of priorities. The media advertises the convenience of ready meals and the ease of one-click delivery services, so the temptation to avoid gazing into our cupboards and planning a meal is never far away.

Deciding what to cook is often the greatest challenge. I believe that anybody is capable of cooking simple and delicious food, but coming up with meal ideas is another matter. Recipes touted as 'quick and easy' often have extensive ingredient lists and require all manner of kitchen equipment, providing little inclination for most home cooks.

Good Food Fast aims to fill that gap by providing both inspiration and ease of access to wonderful, quick food. Out of the 80 recipes, three-quarters take just 30 minutes to prepare and cook. These dishes are fantastic for quick lunches, speedy mid-week meals and desserts to soothe away a bad day at work. The remainder take up to 40 minutes, with that little bit more time and effort focused on relaxed evening meals, weekend events and other occasions that call for special treatment.

Although time is of the essence in this book, it also reflects the shift in what people now like to cook and eat. The movement towards more plant-based diets and mindful meat consumption is recognised throughout. Over half the recipes are vegetarian or vegan, and meals are often centred around vegetables, grains and pulses, rather than the traditional fillet of meat or fish. So balanced nutrition and ethical eating are also a focus.

To further assist the cook, the chapters are arranged by type of dish and cooking method, rather than by individual course. You may seek out the Feasts chapter when entertaining, for example, or head to Salads when something light and fresh is called for. There are no complicated techniques or methods and the recipes were developed in my small home kitchen, often while my baby slept upstairs.

The book begins with a chapter on soups; these often need a bit of preparatory chopping but require little attention once they are simmering away. As with all the chapters, the recipes in Soups are intended to take you through the seasons, providing meal inspiration for all times of the year. Bright, summery recipes, such as a zippy and wholesome Chicken and Lemon Orzo Soup

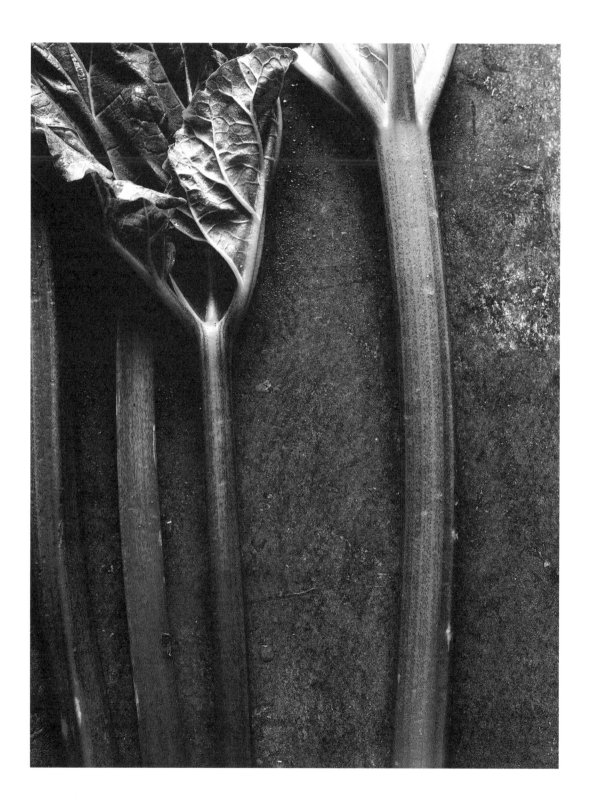

(page 14) and a vibrant Corn and Chorizo Chowder (page 16), are for the summer months; bolstering recipes, such as Mushroom Stroganoff Soup (page 21) and Sweet Potato Curry Noodle Soup (page 23), demonstrate twists on familiar recipes and ways to utilise simple ingredients that the reader may not previously have considered. Textural contrast is also important when serving soups, so in this chapter you'll find pine nuts toasted in balsamic vinegar until sticky and sweet to top a vivid green Rocket and Potato Soup (page 17), and kale baked with sesame, sugar and salt to add depth and crunch to an umami-rich Carrot, Miso and Ginger Soup (page 20).

The Salads chapter is again guided by the seasons, but not slavishly so. The Asparagus, Sugar Snaps and Burrata with Brown Butter Dressing (page 34) is best eaten during the summer months, when the vibrancy of the core ingredients isn't dulled by air miles, but the Coronation Egg Salad (page 41) and the Quick Chicken Caesar Salad with Parmesan Croutes (page 48) can be enjoyed year-round. There are recipes in this chapter that are light but warming, as well as those which require no heat for when it's too hot to even contemplate standing at the stove. Whichever season they sit in, the salads are all satisfying meals in

themselves with an emphasis on enhancing light ingredients with punchy, robust dressings and interesting flavour combinations. Care has been taken to ensure that the salads are not too preparation-heavy, as no one would wish to be chopping for 30 minutes straight. You might need to snap some asparagus, shave the kernels off a corn cob and finely crush some garlic, but that's about as complex as the techniques get.

The Lunches & Lighter Bites chapter is made up of dishes that can be enjoyed at any time of day – quick and straightforward recipes that make for convenient yet delicious mid-week lunches, or even late breakfasts at the weekend. Roasted Broccoli, Caper and Walnut Linguine (page 66) is a popular choice in my house, and is one of those flavour-packed pasta recipes that just so happens to be vegan. Roast Mushroom Gnocchi with Rocket Pesto (page 70) is pure winter comfort in a bowl, while Pea and Ricotta Fritters with Crispy Eggs (page 61) is a fabulous brunch-style dish that the whole family will love – as attested by my one-year-old.

The One Pots & Traybakes chapter utilises the simplest cooking methods in order to create delicious, low-effort food. These recipes involve little preparation and let the oven or hob do the heavy lifting. The ingredients for the Oregano Lamb and Pistachio Traybake (page 83), for example, are simply put together and roasted in two stages, allowing the flavours to meld and infuse as they roast. Cooked over a gentle heat on the stove, the Red Pepper and Butter Bean Eggs (page 90) can gently bubble away, leaving breathing room and time to attend to other things while cooking. These recipes will, hopefully, become weeknight saviours and the go-to for when you're just too busy, or tired, to face the kitchen.

In the Feasts chapter, you'll find 40-minute recipes for when you have a little bit more time for cooking. Full of hearty dishes, ranging from simple and comforting to modern and exciting, this chapter reveals shortcuts to stews and bakes, as well as showcasing easy ways to use more unusual supermarket ingredients. Roasted Togarashi Salmon with Citrus Sesame Dressing (page 109) is one such dish, and is both impressive for guests and accessible for the cook. It uses the Japanese spice mix, shichimi togarashi, to impart a gently spiced umami kick to the salmon. The dish is finished with a take on a citrussy Japanese sesame dressing, which uses easily accessible tahini in place of Japanese sesame paste. Another favourite for entertaining are the Crab Tostadas with Pea Guacamole and Pickled

Shallots (page 104): a twist on a Mexican classic perfect for sunny evenings with friends.

Finally, on to Desserts. A truly quick dessert may seem particularly elusive but, in this chapter, you'll find an Apricot and Pistachio Danish Pastry Tart (page 129), Peanut Butter French Toast (page 133) and Banoffee Puddings (page 139) – all ready in 40 minutes or less. These bakes require no special equipment, apart from electric whisks, and make for perfect desserts and tea-time treats. There are several recipes that require chilling or freezing, such as the Malted Milk Chocolate Affogato (page 142) and the Pineapple Sorbet with Lime and Mint (page 130), but the preparation time for both is minimal.

My hope is that *Good Food Fast* will become a trusted kitchen companion, providing access to wholesome, delicious food that fits into busy lives.

Soups

Chicken and Lemon Orzo Soup

This light, comforting soup has all the key flavours of a traditional chicken soup, with the added brightness of lemon juice and dill. Be sure to add the lemon juice right at the end – cooking the lemon will impair its fresh flavour. Use any leftover dill in the Beetroot, Radish and Grapefruit Salad (see page 54).

SERVES: 4 | PREP TIME: 10 mins | COOKING TIME: 30 mins

25g (1oz) butter
1 medium onion,
   peeled and finely
   chopped
1 large carrot, peeled
   and finely chopped
1 rib of celery,
   trimmed and finely
   chopped
2 garlic cloves
½ a small bunch
   of parsley
4 boneless chicken
   thighs
1 litre (1¾ pints)
   chicken stock
75g (3oz) orzo
2 sprigs of dill
Juice of ½ a lemon

Melt the butter in a large saucepan. Once foaming, add the onion, carrot and celery. Cover and cook gently for 6 minutes, stirring now and then, until slightly softened.

While the vegetables are cooking, peel and crush the garlic. Finely chop the parsley stalks and roughly chop the leaves. Cut the chicken thighs in half.

Add the garlic and parsley stalks to the softened vegetables. Cook for 1 minute and then add the chicken and cook for a further minute or two, until sealed. Pour over the stock and simmer for 15–18 minutes, adding the orzo for the final 10 minutes of cooking. Pick the dill fronds from their stalks.

Remove the chicken from the pan and shred roughly with two forks. Season the soup to taste and add the parsley leaves, dill and lemon juice to serve.

Corn and Chorizo Chowder

A twist on an American classic; in this recipe, the sweetness of the corn is tempered with smoky, savoury chorizo. Be sure to use cooking chorizo, which you'll find in the chilled section at the supermarket. Use up any remaining chives in the Herby Chard and Gruyère Frittata (see page 58).

SERVES: 4 | PREP TIME: 10 mins | COOKING TIME: 20 mins

2 tsp olive oil

125g (4oz) cooking chorizo, diced

1 rib of celery, trimmed and finely diced

4 spring onions, trimmed and finely diced

1 medium potato

1½ tbsp plain flour

2 sprigs of thyme

500ml (17fl oz) whole milk

400ml (14fl oz) chicken or vegetable stock

A small bunch of chives

200g (7oz) frozen corn

Add the oil and chorizo to a large pan and cook over a low to medium heat for 5 minutes, until golden and slightly crisp.

Remove half the chorizo with a slotted spoon and set aside on some kitchen towel. Add the celery and spring onions to the pan and cook for a further 4 minutes, until just softened.

Peel and cut the potato into 1cm (⅜in) dice.

Add the flour to the pan, cook for 1 minute and then add the potato, thyme, milk and stock. Bring up to a boil and simmer for 8–10 minutes, until the potato is just tender but still holding its shape. Keep an eye on the soup as milk has a tendency to boil over. Finely chop the chives.

Tip the corn into the soup, bring up to the boil and season to taste. Discard the thyme. Serve topped with the chives and reserved chorizo.

Rocket and Potato Soup with Balsamic Pine Nuts

With a humble backbone of shallots, potatoes and garlic, this soup is enlivened by bright and peppery rocket, a dash of lemon juice and salty Parmesan. Finish with sweet balsamic pine nuts (also fantastic as a snack) for a little crunch. Vegetarian or vegan alternatives to Parmesan are available in all large supermarkets.

SERVES: 4 | EQUIPMENT: Blender | PREP TIME: 5 mins | COOKING TIME: 25 mins

2 echalion shallots
1½ tbsp olive oil
4 garlic cloves
500g (1lb 2oz) floury potatoes (such as Maris Piper)
1 litre (1¾ pints) vegetable stock
30g (1¼oz) pine nuts
2 tsp balsamic vinegar
30g (1¼oz) Parmesan or vegetarian alternative
1 lemon
150g (5oz) rocket

Peel and finely slice the shallots. Heat the oil in a large saucepan, add the shallots and cook gently for 6–8 minutes, until softened.

Meanwhile, peel and crush the garlic. Peel and halve the potatoes lengthways. Finely slice.

Add the garlic to the pan and cook for 1 minute, until fragrant. Stir in the potatoes and stock and simmer for 12–15 minutes, until the potatoes are tender.

Meanwhile, toast the pine nuts in a dry pan for 1–2 minutes, until lightly golden. Add the balsamic vinegar and allow to bubble away, moving the pine nuts from time to time, until sticky. Set aside for now.

Finely grate the Parmesan. Slice the lemon in half. Add the rocket to the soup in handfuls and stir to wilt. Blend until smooth and season, adding lemon juice to taste. Top with the pine nuts to finish.

Black Bean and Tomato Chipotle Soup

This piquant and wholesome Mexican soup is given some heat and a mellow, smoky flavour with the addition of chipotle chilli paste. Different brands can vary in strength so start with the smaller recommended amount and add a little more at the end, if liked. Leftover coriander can be used in the Sweet Potato Curry Noodle Soup (see page 23), or the Noodle Salad with Garlic Peanut Dressing (see page 42).

SERVES: 4 | VEGAN | PREP TIME: 5 mins | COOKING TIME: 25 mins

2 tbsp sunflower oil

2 shallots, peeled and finely chopped

1 lime

4 garlic cloves

1 x 400g (14oz) can black beans

2 tsp ground cumin

2 tsp smoked paprika

1–2 tsp chipotle paste

400ml (14fl oz) passata

500ml (17fl oz) vegetable stock

A pinch of sugar

1 avocado

A small bunch of coriander

Heat the oil in a large saucepan. Cook half the shallots gently in the oil for 4–5 minutes, until softened. Juice the lime. Put the remaining shallots in a bowl with the lime juice and a pinch of salt. Set aside until ready to serve.

Peel and crush the garlic. Drain and rinse the beans in a sieve. Add the garlic to the pan with the cumin, paprika and chipotle paste and cook for 1 minute. Add the passata, beans, stock and sugar and bring to the boil. Simmer for 15–20 minutes, until slightly reduced and flavourful.

While the soup is cooking, halve and finely chop the avocado. Roughly chop the coriander.

Check the seasoning of the soup and add more chipotle paste if needed. Ladle into bowls and top with the lime-pickled shallots, avocado and coriander.

Carrot, Miso and Ginger Soup with Sesame Kale

This rich and savoury soup matches the earthy sweetness of carrots with the deep umami of miso. Serve with crunchy, sesame kale for added flavour and texture. In order for the carrots to cook quickly they need to be sliced quite thinly – no thicker than about 0.5cm (¼in).

SERVES: 4 | VEGAN | EQUIPMENT: Blender | PREP TIME: 10 mins | COOKING TIME: 20 mins

100g (3½oz) sliced kale

3 tbsp groundnut or sunflower oil

1 tbsp sesame seeds

A pinch of salt

A pinch of sugar

6 spring onions

500g (1lb 2oz) carrots

1 medium potato

2cm (¾in) piece of ginger

4 garlic cloves

1.2 litres (2 pints) vegetable stock

1 tbsp brown or red miso paste

1 tbsp light soy (or to taste)

Preheat the oven to 180°C / 160°C fan / gas mark 4.

In a bowl, toss the kale with 1 tbsp of the oil, the sesame seeds, salt and sugar. Once the kale is well coated, spread out on a baking tray in a single layer and bake for 15 minutes, turning halfway through cooking, until crisp.

Meanwhile, trim and roughly chop the spring onions. Peel and cut the carrots into thin slices. Peel and finely chop the potato. Peel and finely grate the ginger and garlic.

Heat the remaining oil in a large saucepan. Add the spring onions, garlic and ginger and cook for 2–3 minutes, until softened and fragrant. Stir in the carrots and potato, pour over the stock, cover and simmer for 15 minutes, until the carrots are just tender. Blend until smooth with the miso and soy sauce, to taste.

Serve the soup with the kale on top or to the side.

Mushroom Stroganoff Soup

A livelier version of a classic cream of mushroom, this soup is spiked with smoked paprika and Worcestershire sauce (it's worth seeking out a vegetarian version) and enriched with tart crème fraîche to evoke the flavours of a stroganoff. Use the largest pan you have for the soup; the mushrooms need space to colour and will sweat if overcrowded. Use any leftover parsley in the Celeriac and Apple Salad with Parsley and Almond Dressing (see page 51).

SERVES: 4 | **VEGETARIAN** | **EQUIPMENT:** Blender | **PREP TIME:** 5 mins | **COOKING TIME:** 20 mins

2 shallots
2 tbsp olive oil
500g (1lb 2oz) chestnut
   mushrooms
2 garlic cloves
1 tbsp smoked paprika
2 tbsp plain flour
1 litre (1¾ pints) stock
1 tbsp vegetarian
   Worcestershire
   sauce, or light
   soy sauce
A small bunch
   of parsley
200g (7oz) crème
   fraîche

Peel and finely slice the shallots. Heat the oil in a large saucepan. Add the shallots and cook gently on a low heat for 6–8 minutes, until softened.

Meanwhile, clean and roughly chop the mushrooms. Peel and crush the garlic. Once the shallot is soft, increase the heat and fry the mushrooms for 4–5 minutes, until well coloured. Add the garlic and paprika and cook for 1 minute, until fragrant. Stir in the flour, then add the stock and Worcestershire sauce or soy. Bring up to the boil and simmer for 8 minutes.

While the soup is cooking, roughly chop the parsley. Remove the soup from the heat and blend with the crème fraîche and most of the parsley. Season to taste and sprinkle with the remaining parsley to serve.

Sweet Potato Curry Noodle Soup

This rich and delicately spiced noodle soup is inspired by Khao Soi from Northern Thailand. This quick version of the Thai classic cannot claim to be authentic, but it makes for a vibrant and comforting meal that's ready in a flash. You can use the remainder of the coriander in the Noodle Salad with Garlic Peanut Dressing (see page 42).

SERVES: 4 | VEGAN | PREP TIME: 10 mins | COOKING TIME: 20 mins

1 small red onion

2 limes

1½ tbsp vegetable oil

2cm (¾in) piece
   of ginger

1 large sweet potato

4 tbsp red Thai
   curry paste

2 tsp medium curry
   powder

400ml (14fl oz) can
   coconut milk

500ml (17fl oz)
   vegetable stock

150g (5oz) sugar
   snap peas

A handful of coriander

200g (7oz) flat rice
   noodles

1–2 tbsp light soy
   sauce

Peel and finely slice the red onion. Juice 1 lime and cut the other into wedges. Put half the onion in a small bowl and cover with the lime juice. Set aside while you continue.

Heat 1 tbsp oil, add the remaining onion and cook for 4–5 minutes, until beginning to soften.

Peel and finely grate the ginger. Peel and chop the sweet potato into 1.5cm (½in) cubes. Add the curry paste, curry powder and the ginger to the pan. Cook for 1 minute, stirring occasionally. Add the sweet potato, coconut milk and stock. Simmer gently for 15 minutes, until the potato is just tender.

Meanwhile, slice the sugar snap peas in half on the diagonal. Roughly chop the coriander. Cook the noodles according to pack the instructions. Drain, run under cold water and set aside.

Add the sugar snaps to the soup pan and simmer for 1 minute, until just tender. Taste the soup and season with soy sauce, to your liking.

Divide the noodles between bowls and pour over the soup. Add slices of the pickled onions, coriander and lime wedges to serve.

Smashed Chickpea and Harissa Soup

Crushing the chickpeas releases their natural starches, making for a slightly thicker soup. Harissa pastes tend to vary in intensity and heat so the amount in the recipe is just a guide: start with a tablespoon and adjust according to taste. Try using up any remaining coriander in the Noodle Salad with Garlic Peanut Dressing (see page 42).

SERVES: 4 | VEGAN | PREP TIME: 10 mins | COOKING TIME: 20 mins

2½ tbsp olive oil

2 echalion shallots, peeled and finely sliced

2 celery stalks, trimmed and diced

1 large or 2 small carrots, trimmed and diced

2 garlic cloves

1 x 400g (14oz) can chickpeas

1 tsp ground cumin

1–2 tbsp harissa, plus ¼ tsp

1 x 400g (14oz) can chopped tomatoes

500ml (17fl oz) vegetable stock

A small bunch of coriander

Heat 2 tbsp of the oil in a large saucepan. Add the shallots, celery and carrots and cook for 6–8 minutes, until softened.

Peel and crush the garlic. Drain the chickpeas.

Add the garlic, cumin and harissa to the pan and cook for 1 minute, until fragrant. Pour in the chickpeas, reserving 2 tbsp for the topping. Crush with a fork to break up slightly, then pour in the chopped tomatoes and stock. Bring up to the boil and simmer for 10 minutes.

Meanwhile, roughly chop the coriander. Heat the remaining oil in a small frying pan and add the rest of the harissa and chickpeas. Fry for 3–4 minutes, until crisp.

Season the soup to taste and serve with the coriander and crispy chickpeas.

Squash and Chestnut Soup

This silky, nutty soup is perfectly warming for chilly days. It's also a great way to use up leftover chestnuts from Christmas. The soup is rich enough in itself, but a splash of oat or vegan cream of your choice adds a luxurious depth. You can use up any remaining sage in the Butternut, Sage and Hazelnut Orzotto (see page 94).

SERVES: 4 | VEGAN | EQUIPMENT: Blender | PREP TIME: 5 mins | COOKING TIME: 30–35 mins

2 echalion shallots

3 tbsp olive oil

1 butternut squash – about 1kg (2lb 3oz)

2 garlic cloves

1 litre (1¾ pints) vegetable stock

200g (7oz) ready-cooked chestnuts

4 sage leaves

A pinch of chilli flakes

A splash of vegan cream (optional)

Peel, halve and finely slice the shallots. Heat 2 tbsp of the oil in a large saucepan. Add the shallots and cook gently for 6–8 minutes, to soften.

Peel, deseed and chop the squash into 2cm (¾in) chunks. Peel and crush the garlic. Add the garlic to the pan and cook for 1 minute. Add the squash, followed by the stock. Bring up to the boil and simmer for 15–20 minutes, until the squash is tender.

Meanwhile, finely chop the chestnuts. Add most to the pan for the last 5 minutes, reserving a handful for the topping.

Finely chop the sage leaves. Heat the remaining oil in a frying pan and add the chestnuts, sage and chilli flakes. Fry gently for 4–5 minutes, until crisp and golden.

Blend the soup until smooth. Season to taste and stir through a dash of cream, if liked. Serve sprinkled with the chestnut crumb.

Shiitake Rice Soup

This gentle and soothing soup is a speedy take on Chinese congee: a delicately fragranced, slow-cooked rice porridge. This quick version differs in texture but the flavours shine through, in spite of the short cooking time. I like the fragrance of jasmine rice but basmati would also work well.

SERVES: 4 | VEGAN | PREP TIME: 10 mins | COOKING TIME: 20 mins

15g (½oz) dried
   shiitake or porcini
   mushrooms
4 spring onions
2cm (¾in) piece
   of ginger
100g (3½oz) shiitake
   mushrooms
2½ tbsp groundnut
   or sunflower oil
150g (5oz) jasmine rice
1 litre (1¾ pints)
   vegetable stock
1½ tbsp soy sauce
2 pak choi
2 garlic cloves
Chilli oil, to serve

Cover the dried mushrooms in boiling water and set aside. Trim and finely slice the spring onions. Peel and slice the ginger into thin matchsticks. Clean and slice the fresh mushrooms.

Heat 1 tbsp of the oil in a large saucepan and add most of the spring onions and ginger, saving a little for serving. Cook gently for 2 minutes, until beginning to soften. Add half the mushrooms and cook for a further 2–3 minutes.

Briefly rinse the rice and add to the pan with the stock, dried mushrooms and their soaking liquor and soy sauce. Bring up to the boil and simmer for 10–12 minutes, until the rice is tender.

While the rice is cooking, slice the pak choi. Peel and slice the garlic. Heat the remaining oil in a large frying pan and add the rest of the mushrooms. Fry for 2 minutes, until golden. Add the garlic and cook for 1–2 minutes, until fragrant and lightly coloured.

Stir the pak choi stalks into the soup and simmer for 1 minute, until tender. Add the leafy ends. Serve the soup topped with the fried mushrooms and garlic, the remaining ginger and spring onions. Drizzle over chilli oil, if liked.

Roast Cauliflower and Hazelnut Soup

Cauliflower has soared in popularity in recent years. No longer just for boiling and cloaking in cheese sauce, this versatile brassica has a multitude of uses. I like to roast it to bring out its sweet nuttiness. Here, it is quickly roasted with hazelnuts and blended to a thick, comforting soup. Preheat the oven whilst you prep the ingredients to save time.

SERVES: 4 | VEGAN | EQUIPMENT: Blender | PREP TIME: 5 mins |
COOKING TIME: 25 mins

1 large cauliflower
2 echalion shallots
4 sprigs of thyme
2 tbsp olive oil
2 cloves garlic
30g (1¼oz) blanched
 hazelnuts
800ml (28fl oz)
 vegetable stock
½ a small bunch of
 parsley, roughly
 chopped

Preheat the oven to 220°C / 200°C fan / gas mark 7.

Trim the cauliflower and cut into small florets, reserving any smaller leaves. Peel and halve the shallots.

Tip the cauliflower and shallots into a large roasting tin with the thyme sprigs. Season to taste, pour over the oil and stir through until everything is well coated. Roast for 15–20 minutes, until golden and tender.

Meanwhile, peel and crush the garlic. 5 minutes from the end of cooking, stir the garlic through the cauliflower. Add the hazelnuts to a separate baking tray and place in the oven for 5 minutes.

Discard the thyme. Transfer the cauliflower and three-quarters of the hazelnuts to a blender with the stock. Blend until smooth and season to taste. Roughly chop the remaining hazelnuts.

Heat the soup, if needed, and serve topped with the parsley and remaining hazelnuts.

Onion, Celeriac and Bacon Soup

Starting the bacon off in cold oil may be counterintuitive, but as the oil warms, it will render the fat slowly, making for crispier bacon. The onion and celeriac are cooked gently in the leftover bacon fat for a deeply savoury soup. Cut through with sharp, creamy crème fraîche and finish with bacon and chive sprinkles. Leftover chives can be used up in the Coronation Egg Salad (see page 41).

SERVES: 4 | EQUIPMENT: Blender | PREP TIME: 5 mins | COOKING TIME: 20–25 mins

6 rashers of
   streaky bacon
1 tbsp olive oil
1 large onion
4 sprigs of thyme
1 celeriac
1.2 litres (2 pints)
   chicken stock
A small bunch
   of chives
100g (3½oz)
   crème fraîche

Finely chop the bacon. Pour the oil into a large saucepan, add the bacon and fry over a medium heat for 4–5 minutes, until crisp. Remove from the pan with a slotted spoon and set aside.

Meanwhile, peel and finely chop the onion. Add the onion and thyme sprigs to the pan and cook gently for 6 minutes, until softened.

Peel and chop the celeriac into 2cm (¾in) chunks. Add to the pan with the stock and simmer for 10–12 minutes, until the celeriac is tender to the tip of a knife.

Finely chop the chives. Add the crème fraîche to the soup and blend until smooth. Season to taste and serve with the bacon and chives sprinkled over the top.

Summer Tortellini Minestrone

This cannot claim to be an authentic minestrone, but rather is inspired by the comforting Italian soup. It is a light, summery broth studded with seasonal vegetables and finished with tortellini, making it super simple to prepare. The quality of the soup will be a reflection of the ingredients, so try to seek out the best-quality vegetarian fresh tortellini that you can. Use any leftover basil in the Corn and Courgette Salad with a Smoky Tomato Dressing (see page 35).

SERVES: 4 | VEGETARIAN | PREP TIME: 10 mins | COOKING TIME: 18–20 mins

2 tbsp olive oil
4 spring onions, peeled and finely sliced
1 leek, trimmed and finely sliced
4 garlic cloves
1 medium carrot
1 litre (1¾ pints) vegetable stock
200g (7oz) asparagus
30g (1¼oz) vegetarian Italian hard cheese
A handful of basil leaves
250g (9oz) pack vegetarian tortellini (I used spinach and ricotta)
150g (5oz) frozen peas
Crusty bread, to serve

Heat the oil in a large saucepan. Add the spring onion and leek and cook gently for 4–5 minutes, until beginning to soften.

Peel and crush the garlic. Peel and finely chop the carrot. Add the garlic to the pan, cook for 1 minute, then stir in the carrot. Pour over the stock and simmer gently for 10 minutes.

Meanwhile, after trimming and discarding the woody ends, cut the asparagus into pieces 2cm (¾in) long. Finely grate the cheese. Tear the basil leaves.

Add the asparagus, tortellini and peas to the pan. Simmer for 2–3 minutes, until the vegetables and pasta are tender with a little bite. Season to taste and serve with the cheese and some crusty bread.

Salads

Asparagus, Sugar Snaps and Burrata with Brown Butter Dressing

A fresh spring salad of asparagus, sugar snap peas and mint is enriched with creamy burrata and a lemon and brown butter dressing. Browning the butter caramelises the milk solids, giving them a sweet and nutty flavour. Keep a close eye on it because if it's taken too far it will taste bitter. Use any leftover mint in the Roasted Chickpeas and Cauliflower on Garlic and Mint Yogurt (see page 95).

SERVES: 4 | VEGETARIAN | PREP TIME: 15 mins | COOKING TIME: 6–8 mins

400g (14oz) asparagus
200g (7oz) sugar
  snap peas
A few sprigs of mint
1 lemon
40g (1½oz) hazelnuts
40g (1½oz) salted
  butter
1 tbsp olive oil
100g (3½oz) rocket
1 x 200g (7oz)
  ball burrata

Snap the woody ends from the asparagus. Halve the sugar snaps on the diagonal. Pick the leaves from the mint. Juice the lemon.

Roughly chop the hazelnuts. Heat a frying pan and add the hazelnuts. Dry fry for 2–3 minutes, until golden. Add the butter to the pan and allow to melt. Keep an eye on the butter and, once it is golden and smells biscuity, remove from the heat and add the lemon juice. Season to taste. Pour out of the pan and set aside.

Heat the oil in the pan. Once very hot, add the asparagus and fry for 3–4 minutes, adding the sugar snaps for the final minute, until bright green and blistered. Transfer to a salad bowl and toss with the rocket. Top with the burrata, pour over the dressing and finish with the mint.

Corn and Courgette Salad with a Smoky Tomato Dressing

This high-summer salad celebrates the sweet creaminess of corn and courgette by serving them raw with a tangy tomato, lime and smoked paprika dressing. The corn and courgette both need to be very fresh; if you can seek out corn with the husk, even better. You can use up any leftover herbs in the White Bean and Anchovy Salad with Salsa Verde (see page 50).

SERVES: 4 | **VEGETARIAN** | **EQUIPMENT:** Blender | **PREP TIME:** 20 mins

1 garlic clove, crushed

4 sundried tomatoes in oil

1 lime

1 tsp maple syrup

1 tsp smoked paprika

2 courgettes

2 corn on the cob

4 spring onions

A small bunch of parsley

A handful of basil

Begin by making the dressing. Peel and crush the garlic. Drain the sundried tomatoes, reserving 2 tbsp of the oil. Roughly chop the tomatoes. Juice the lime and blend with the oil, garlic, tomatoes, maple syrup and paprika, until fairly smooth. Loosen with a little water to achieve a pourable consistency. Season to taste.

Use a vegetable peeler to slice the courgette into ribbons. Discard the seedy core. Carefully slice the kernels off the corn. Trim and finely slice the spring onions. Roughly chop the parsley and tear the basil leaves. Transfer all of the chopped ingredients to a salad bowl and drizzle over the dressing to finish.

Crab and Mango Salad with Tamarind

Perfect for summer entertaining, this salad is a wonderful combination of sweet, sour and salty, with a gentle buzz of heat. Crab meat isn't cheap but you will probably find the best value at your local fishmonger. I've suggested using white meat, but if you like the rich butteriness of brown meat, use a combination of the two. Leftover basil can be used in the Corn and Courgette Salad With a Smoky Tomato Dressing (see page 35), and coriander in the Coronation Egg Salad (see page 41).

SERVES: 4 | PREP TIME: 20 mins | COOKING TIME: 2–3 mins

40g (1½oz) roasted and salted peanuts

1 ripe mango

4 spring onions

1 red chilli

A small bunch of basil

A small bunch of coriander

2 tbsp tamarind paste

2 tbsp runny honey

1½ tbsp fish sauce or light soy sauce

2 limes

1 tbsp groundnut oil

100g (3½oz) baby spinach

100g (3½oz) white crab meat

Heat a small frying pan and dry fry the peanuts for 2–3 minutes, until golden. Remove from the pan and set aside.

Peel the mango, cut the flesh away from the stone and slice. Trim and finely slice the spring onions. Finely slice the chilli. Pick the leaves from the basil. Roughly chop the coriander. Once the peanuts have cooled, roughly chop.

To make the dressing, mix together the tamarind, honey and fish sauce or soy. Squeeze the limes, add to the dressing with the oil and stir to combine.

Toss together the spinach, mango, spring onions, chilli and herbs. Top with the crab, spoon over the dressing and sprinkle over the peanuts to serve.

Artichoke Panzanella

This Tuscan tomato and bread salad celebrates the peak of tomato season, whilst also rejuvenating day-old bread. Traditionally, the bread is left to soak up the tomato juices until soft. In this salad, though, ciabatta is roughly torn and baked into crisp, garlicky croutons to provide texture and crunch. Any leftover basil can be used in the White Bean and Anchovy Salad with Salsa Verde (see page 50).

SERVES: 4 | VEGETARIAN | PREP TIME: 20 mins | COOKING TIME: 10 mins

200g (7oz) day-old sourdough or ciabatta, torn into rough chunks
60ml (2fl oz) extra-virgin olive oil
1 garlic clove, peeled and crushed
750g (1lb 10oz) ripe tomatoes
1 shallot
2½ tbsp red wine vinegar
2 tbsp capers
30g (1¼oz) vegetarian Italian hard cheese
175g (6oz) marinated artichokes
A handful of basil leaves

Preheat the oven to 200°C / 180°C fan / gas mark 6.

Spread the bread out onto a large baking tray. Toss with 1 tbsp of the oil and season. Bake for 10 minutes, stirring through the garlic for the final 2 minutes, until crisp and golden.

Meanwhile, quarter any large tomatoes and halve any smaller ones. Sprinkle over a little salt and sit in a colander for 10 minutes. Peel and finely slice the shallot and add to a bowl with the vinegar. Roughly chop the capers. Shave the cheese with a vegetable peeler.

Drain the artichokes and fold through the bread, tomatoes, capers and basil leaves. Drizzle over the remaining oil, along with the vinegar and shallot mixture. Finish with the cheese shavings and serve.

Coronation Egg Salad

This vegetarian twist on classic Coronation Chicken makes for a fantastic lunch or light meal. You want the egg yolks to be fudgy in texture; be sure to set a timer and plunge the eggs into cold water after boiling to avoid overcooking. Serve with plenty of watercress and crusty bread – any leftovers can be used up in sandwiches. Use leftover coriander in the Spring Greens and Spiced Tomato Dal (see page 100).

SERVES: 4 | VEGETARIAN | PREP TIME: 15 mins | COOKING TIME: 8–9 mins

6 medium eggs
4 spring onions
A small handful
   of coriander
A small bunch
   of chives
3 tbsp mayonnaise
2 tbsp Greek yogurt
2 tsp medium curry
   powder
2 tbsp mango chutney
85–100g (3½oz)
   watercress
25g (1oz) toasted
   flaked almonds
Crusty bread, to serve

Lower the eggs into a large pan of boiling water and simmer for 8 minutes from room temperature or 9 minutes from fridge cold. Once the time has elapsed, immediately plunge into ice-cold water to stop the eggs from cooking any further.

Meanwhile, trim and finely slice the spring onions. Roughly chop the coriander and finely chop the chives. Mix together the mayonnaise, yogurt, curry powder, chutney and half the herbs. Season to taste and loosen with 1 tbsp cold water, to make a thick dressing.

Peel the eggs and slice into quarters. Season to taste and lay on top of the watercress. Drizzle over the dressing and finish with the remaining herbs and the flaked almonds. Serve with crusty bread.

Noodle Salad with Garlic Peanut Dressing

This bright and crunchy noodle salad is perfect for a hot summer's day. It requires minimal effort but delivers on flavour and texture. Peanut butters tend to vary in consistency, so you may need to water the dressing down a little, until pourable. Use up any remaining coriander in the Sweet Potato Curry Noodle Soup (see page 23), and mint in the Beetroot, Radish and Grapefruit Salad (see page 54).

SERVES: 4 | VEGAN | PREP TIME: 30 mins | COOKING TIME: 6 mins

125g (4oz) fine
  rice noodles
2 medium carrots
2 medium courgettes
4 spring onions
1 garlic clove
A small bunch
  of coriander
4 sprigs of mint
2 tbsp peanuts
1 lime
2 tbsp soy sauce
3 tbsp peanut butter
2 tbsp sweet chilli
  sauce

Soak the noodles in a bowl of boiling hot water for 5–6 minutes, until just tender. Drain into a sieve, rinse with cold water and set aside.

Peel the carrots and coarsely grate, along with the courgettes. Trim and finely slice the spring onions. Peel and crush the garlic. Roughly chop the coriander and finely shred the mint leaves. Roughly chop the peanuts.

To make the dressing, juice the lime and mix with the garlic, soy sauce, peanut butter and sweet chilli sauce. Toss with the noodles, vegetables and herbs. Top with the peanuts and serve.

Halloumi, Watermelon and Sumac Salad

Salty halloumi and the tartness of sumac are tempered by sweet and juicy watermelon and a fresh lemon dressing in this Greek salad of sorts. Halloumi is best eaten warm, while it is still soft and creamy, so be sure to serve the salad soon after frying the cheese. Any leftover mint can be used in the Pineapple Sorbet with Lime and Mint (see page 130).

SERVES: 4 | VEGETARIAN | PREP TIME: 15 mins | COOKING TIME: 2–4 mins

1kg (2lb 3oz)
    watermelon
    (½ a medium
    melon)
½ a red onion
16 kalamata olives
1 lemon
4 tbsp olive oil
A large bunch
    of parsley
4 sprigs of mint
1 x 250g (9oz) pack
    halloumi
½ tsp sumac
Pitta bread, to serve

Remove the flesh from the watermelon and roughly slice. Peel and finely slice the onion. Halve the olives. Finely grate the zest and juice the lemon. Mix with the oil, season to taste and pour half over the watermelon, onion and olives.

Roughly chop the parsley, stalks and all. Finely shred the mint leaves. Drain and thinly slice the halloumi.

Heat a large, non-stick frying pan. Dry fry the halloumi for 1–2 minutes each side, until golden.

Lay the halloumi over the watermelon and pour over the remaining dressing, followed by the herbs and the sumac. Serve with warm pitta bread.

Japanese-style Slaw with Carrot Miso Dressing

This peppery, tart and umami-rich slaw takes a bit of preparation but is well worth the effort. The salad is perfectly sufficient on its own but could be served with fried tempeh to make it even more substantial. The dressing needs to be smooth, so blending is essential.

SERVES: 4 | VEGAN | EQUIPMENT: Blender | PREP TIME: 25 mins | COOKING TIME: 5 mins

3 carrots
1 shallot
2cm (¾in) piece
  of ginger
1 tbsp maple syrup
1 tbsp miso paste
3 tbsp rice vinegar
2 tsp sesame oil
2 tbsp groundnut oil
200g (7oz) edamame
  beans
½ a red cabbage
4 spring onions

Peel the carrots and roughly chop one. Peel and roughly chop the shallot and ginger. To make the dressing, put the chopped carrot, shallot, ginger, maple syrup, miso, rice vinegar, sesame oil and the groundnut oil into a blender. Blitz until fine and pourable. Season to taste.

Simmer the edamame beans in boiling water for 4–5 minutes, until just tender with a little bite. Drain into a sieve and run under cold water to cool. Remove the tough core of the cabbage with a deep triangular cut. Discard the core and finely shred the cabbage. Coarsely grate the remaining carrot. Trim and finely slice the spring onions.

Combine the edamame beans with the cabbage, carrot and spring onions. Pour over the dressing and serve.

Roasted Grape, Goats Cheese and Lentil Salad

Roasting grapes brings out their raisiny sweetness and makes them a wonderful match for sharp, creamy goats cheese and nutty lentils. Combine with bitter chicory, peppery leaves and plenty of parsley to make a robust winter salad. Any leftover parsley can be used in the Roast Cauliflower and Hazelnut Soup (see page 28).

SERVES: 4 | VEGETARIAN | PREP TIME: 5 mins | COOKING TIME: 20–25 mins

150g (5oz) Puy lentils

250g (9oz) red seedless grapes

3 tbsp extra-virgin olive oil

1½ tbsp balsamic vinegar

40g (1½oz) walnuts

½ a small bunch of parsley

100g (3½oz) rocket

80g (3¼oz) soft goats cheese

Preheat the oven to 200°C / 180°C fan / gas mark 6.

Rinse the lentils in a sieve. Transfer to a large pan, cover with water and simmer for 20–25 minutes, until tender but with a little bite.

While the lentils are cooking, pick the grapes from their stalks and add to a roasting tin with 1 tbsp of the olive oil and 1 tsp of the vinegar. Season and roast for 10–12 minutes, until slightly softened and juicy. Add the walnuts to a separate tray and roast for 5 minutes.

Meanwhile, whisk the remaining oil and vinegar together. Season to taste. Roughly chop the parsley and walnuts. Drain the lentils, rinse briefly under cold water and place in a large salad bowl. Gently fold through the rocket and grapes. Crumble over the goats cheese. Sprinkle over the parsley and walnuts and pour over the dressing to serve.

Quick Chicken Caesar Salad with Parmesan Croutes

Quickly roasting the chicken and bacon together saves on time and washing up. Simply prepare the dressing and leaves while the chicken cooks and add the croutes towards the end of cooking. Any leftover dressing can be kept in the fridge for two days.

SERVES: 4 | EQUIPMENT: Pestle and mortar or blender | PREP TIME: 10 mins | COOKING TIME: 20 mins

4 skin-on chicken breasts
8 rashers of streaky bacon
2½ tbsp olive oil
1 medium baguette
30g (1¼oz) Parmesan
1 garlic clove
4 anchovy fillets in oil
1 tbsp Dijon mustard
3 tbsp mayonnaise
½ a lemon
2 little gem lettuces

Preheat the oven to 200°C / 180°C fan / gas mark 6.

Season the chicken well and place in a roasting tin. Drape the bacon over the chicken, drizzle with ½ tbsp of the oil and roast for 15 minutes.

Meanwhile, cut the baguette into 8 slices, on the diagonal. Brush with the remaining oil. Grate the Parmesan and sprinkle half over the baguette slices.

Peel and crush the garlic. Place in a pestle and mortar or blender and combine with the anchovy fillets, until paste-like. Stir in the mustard, mayonnaise and the juice from ½ a lemon. Season to taste.

Once the chicken has roasted for 15 minutes, add the croutes, cheese-side up, and roast for a further 5 minutes.

Separate the leaves from the little gem and place in a salad bowl. Add the dressing and toss to combine. Slice the chicken and serve on the salad with the bacon and croutes.

White Bean and Anchovy Salad with Salsa Verde

A simple but flavourful salad that is far greater than the sum of its parts. Made almost entirely of store-cupboard ingredients, a bright and zippy dressing, comprising fresh herbs, capers and lemon keeps things fresh. Be sure to rinse the beans well in a sieve to remove any residue from the tin. Use up any leftover herbs in the Corn and Courgette Salad with a Smoky Tomato Dressing (see page 35).

SERVES: 4 | PREP TIME: 20 mins

1 small red onion, peeled and finely sliced

1 garlic clove, peeled and crushed

Juice of 1 lemon

2 cornichons

4 anchovy fillets, drained

2 tbsp capers, drained

1 small bunch of flat-leaf parsley

1 small bunch of basil

1½ tsp Dijon mustard

3 tbsp olive oil

2 x 400g (14oz) cans cannellini beans

75g (3oz) semi-dried tomatoes

Mix the onion and garlic with the lemon juice and a pinch of salt. Set aside while you continue.

Finely chop the cornichons and anchovies. Roughly chop the capers and parsley. Shred about half the basil leaves.

Spoon the liquid off the onions and combine with the mustard, oil, chopped herbs, cornichons, capers and anchovies to make a thick dressing. Season to taste.

Drain the beans and rinse well in a sieve. Toss with the tomatoes and onions and pour over the dressing. Top with the reserved basil and serve.

Celeriac and Apple Salad with Parsley and Almond Dressing

Fresh and crisp, the nuttiness of celeriac is brought to life with rich almonds in this twist on a remoulade, cut through with green apples and lemon for balance. It's important to make the dressing first to keep the colour of the celeriac and apples. Use up any leftover parsley in the Roasted Grape, Goats Cheese and Lentil Salad (see page 47).

SERVES: 4 | VEGAN | PREP TIME: 25 mins | COOKING TIME: 3–4 mins

40g (1½oz) whole
   almonds
1 lemon
3 tbsp almond butter
1½ tbsp Dijon mustard
½ a celeriac
2 green apples
A large handful
   of parsley
80g (3¼oz) lambs
   lettuce

Roughly chop the almonds. Toast in a dry frying pan over a medium heat for 2–3 minutes, until golden. Remove from the pan and set aside.

Juice the lemon into a large salad bowl and mix in the almond butter and mustard. Add 1–2 tbsp of water to loosen the dressing slightly (you're looking for a similar thickness to natural yogurt). Season to taste.

Peel and coarsely grate the celeriac. Tip directly into the bowl and toss in the dressing, to coat. Coarsely grate the apple and combine with the celeriac. Taste the salad and adjust the seasoning.

Roughly chop the parsley and add to the bowl with the lambs lettuce. Coat in the dressing and serve topped with the toasted almonds.

Clementine, Chicory and Pomegranate Salad

This crisp, zesty salad is a wonderful way to brighten up dull winter days with interesting textures and jewel-like colours. To open the pomegranate, slice the stem of the fruit off to reveal the sections of the seeds. Make incisions around the fruit at each section of membrane and pull open the skin to release the whole seeds.

SERVES: 4 | VEGAN | PREP TIME: 30 mins

200g (7oz) bulgur wheat
1 small pomegranate
4 spring onions
4 clementines
2 heads of red chicory
40g (1½oz) pistachios
Juice of 1 lemon
3 tbsp olive oil
1 tbsp pomegranate molasses
60g (2¼oz) watercress

Rinse the bulgur wheat in a sieve and transfer to a bowl. Pour over enough boiling water to cover the grains by 2cm (¾in), cover and set aside to soak for 25 minutes.

Break open the pomegranate to remove the seeds. Finely slice the spring onions. Peel the clementines and cut crosswise into slices 1cm (⅜in) thick. Trim the roots of the chicory and separate the leaves. Roughly chop the pistachios.

Mix the lemon juice with the oil and pomegranate molasses. Season to taste.

Fluff the bulgur wheat to taste and season. Toss with the pomegranate, spring onions, chicory and watercress. Serve with the slices of clementine and top with the dressing and pistachios.

Beetroot, Radish and Grapefruit Salad

The mouth-puckeringly sharp, sweet dressing for this salad brings the earthy flavour of beetroot to life. Slicing the beetroot takes a bit of time; coarsely grating them will make the salad even quicker to bring together.

SERVES: 4 | VEGAN | PREP TIME: 30 mins

1 red grapefruit
1 tsp light brown
    soft sugar
3 tbsp olive oil
1 red onion
100g (3½oz) radishes
4 beetroots (different
    colours, if you can
    find them)
A bunch each of
    parsley, mint
    and dill
A pinch of chilli flakes
½ tsp sumac

Finely zest and juice the grapefruit. Mix the juice with the sugar and olive oil to make a dressing. Peel and finely slice the onion and toss with the dressing. Season well.

Finely slice the radishes. Peel and finely slice the beetroot using a sharp knife or mandolin. Roughly chop the herbs.

Combine the radishes, beetroot and herbs with the dressing, and sprinkle with the chilli flakes and sumac to finish.

Lunches & Light Bites

Herby Chard and Gruyère Frittata

Earthy and slightly sweet, Swiss and rainbow chard make wonderful additions to bakes, pasta dishes and, in this case, frittatas. This simple recipe allows the flavour of the chard to shine through, enhanced by nutty Gruyère and herbs. Gruyère uses animal enzymes in the making process so use a vegetarian alternative, if preferred. Use any leftover chives in the Pea and Ricotta Fritters with Crispy Eggs (see page 61).

SERVES: 4 | PREP TIME: 10 mins | COOKING TIME: 15 mins

200g (7oz) rainbow
    or Swiss chard
6 spring onions
20g (¾oz) butter
A small bunch
    of chives
A small bunch
    of parsley
2 sprigs of tarragon
8 eggs
50g (2oz) Gruyère
    (or vegetarian
    alternative)
Green salad, to serve

Separate the chard leaves from the stalks. Chop the stalks and finely shred the leaves. Finely slice the spring onions.

Preheat a grill to high. Melt the butter in a large frying pan. Once foaming, add the chard stalks and spring onions. Cook gently for 4–5 minutes, until softened.

Meanwhile, finely chop the herbs, stalks and all. Beat the eggs and season well. Finely grate the cheese.

Add the chard leaves to the pan and cook for 2 minutes, until wilted. Pour over the eggs, herbs and cheese, stir to combine and cook gently for 3–4 minutes, until the edges are set. Pop the frying pan under the grill for a final 2–3 minutes, until the eggs are just set.

Leave to cool for a few minutes before serving with a green salad.

Hot-smoked Salmon Hash

New potatoes are fried in olive oil and butter until golden and crisp. The hash is cooked with vibrant spring greens and topped with hot-smoked salmon after cooking, to prevent the fish from drying out in the pan. There might be more pickled red onion than you need; use the remainder in salads or over tacos. You can use the rest of the dill in the Beetroot, Radish and Grapefruit Salad (see page 54).

SERVES: 4 | PREP TIME: 5 mins | COOKING TIME: 25 mins

750g (1lb 10oz)
  new potatoes
1 red onion
1 lemon
200g (7oz) spring
  greens
6 cornichons
A small bunch of dill
2 tbsp olive oil
15g (½oz) butter
Approx. 160g (5½oz)
  hot-smoked salmon
Crème fraîche,
  to serve

Halve the potatoes and quarter any larger ones, so that they're all roughly the same size. Boil the potatoes in plenty of salted water for 12–15 minutes, until just tender to the tip of a knife.

Meanwhile, peel, halve and finely chop the onion. Add to a bowl and squeeze over the juice of the lemon.

Remove any tough outer leaves from the spring greens. Separate the leaves, cut out the tough core, roll up into a cigar shape and finely shred. Finely chop the cornichons and roughly chop the dill. Drain the potatoes.

Heat the oil and butter in a large, non-stick frying pan. Add the potatoes and crush lightly with the back of a spatula. Fry for 5–6 minutes, turning occasionally, until crisp at the edges. Add the greens for the final 2 minutes. Season to taste.

Flake the salmon. Once the potatoes are crisp, scatter over the salmon, chopped onion, cornichons and dill. Serve with a dollop of crème fraîche.

Pea and Ricotta Fritters with Crispy Eggs

These light fritters are the perfect vehicle for crisp fried eggs. They freeze brilliantly so if you have a little extra time, make double. To make this recipe even more quickly, use two frying pans and cook two batches of the fritters simultaneously.

SERVES: 4 | EQUIPMENT: Electric whisk | PREP TIME: 15 mins | COOKING TIME: 15 mins

200g (7oz) petits pois
4 spring onions
A small bunch
  of chives
40g (1½oz) Parmesan
  (or vegetarian
  alternative)
6 medium eggs
200g (7oz) ricotta
175ml (6fl oz) milk
150g (5oz) plain flour
1½ tsp baking powder
2 tbsp olive oil, plus
  extra for frying
1 tbsp red wine
  vinegar
85–100g (3½oz)
  pea shoots
Hot sauce, to serve
  (optional)

Preheat the oven to 150°C / 130°C fan / gas mark 2. Cover the petits pois with boiling water and set aside for 2 minutes. Drain and set aside.

Meanwhile, trim and finely slice the spring onions. Finely chop the chives and finely grate the Parmesan.

Separate two of the eggs. Whisk the ricotta, milk and the 2 egg yolks until smooth. In a separate bowl, whisk the egg whites until they hold soft peaks. Fold the flour, baking powder and a good pinch of salt into the ricotta mix. Add the petits pois, spring onions, chives, Parmesan and plenty of black pepper. Fold in the egg whites until just combined.

Wipe a non-stick frying pan with a little oil and add large tablespoons of the ricotta mixture. Cook in batches for 2–3 minutes each side, until risen and golden. Keep warm in the oven. While the fritters are cooking, whisk the remaining oil with the vinegar and season to taste. Toss with the pea shoots.

Heat 1–2 tbsp more oil in the pan. Once very hot, add the four remaining eggs and fry for 2–3 minutes, until the whites are set and crisp at the edges, and the yolks are still runny. Serve the fritters topped with an egg with a portion of dressed pea shoots. Add hot sauce, if liked.

Tenderstem and Romesco Ciabattas

Spanish romesco is a slightly smoky tomato and roasted pepper sauce spiked with vinegar and rounded off with almonds. It is traditionally served with grilled meat, fish or vegetables, but also makes a wonderful addition to a sandwich. In this recipe, it is teamed with roasted tenderstem broccoli and mozzarella and served on ciabatta – fusion at its best.

SERVES: 4 | VEGETARIAN | EQUIPMENT: Blender | PREP TIME: 10 mins | COOKING TIME: 8–10 mins

200g (7oz) tenderstem broccoli
75ml (2½fl oz) olive oil
75g (3oz) blanched almonds
2 garlic cloves
200g (7oz) red peppers from a jar
6 sundried tomatoes
1 tsp smoked paprika
1 tbsp sherry vinegar
4 mini ciabattas
125g (4oz) ball of mozzarella (check that it's vegetarian)

Preheat the oven to 200°C / 180°C fan / gas mark 6.

Trim the broccoli and toss in 1 tbsp of the olive oil. Season to taste and roast in an oven-proof tray for 8–10 minutes, until just tender.

To make the romesco, put the remaining oil and almonds in a blender. Peel the garlic and add that. Drain the peppers and sundried tomatoes and add along with the paprika and vinegar. Blend until smooth. Season to taste.

Split and lightly toast the ciabattas. Drain and slice the mozzarella.

Spread the romesco on the bottom half of each ciabatta. Top with the broccoli and a slice of mozzarella before serving.

Speedy Spelt Pizzas

This quick dough comprises strong white bread flour with wholemeal spelt for a nuttier flavour. This is one of the slightly longer recipes in the book but is far quicker and less laborious than making a traditional dough. Flours often have different levels of absorbency; add enough water to create a soft dough. The toppings here are just a suggestion – anything goes!

MAKES: two 30cm (12in) pizzas | **VEGETARIAN** | **PREP TIME:** 25–30 mins | **COOKING TIME:** 10–12 mins

150g (5oz) wholemeal spelt flour

150g (5oz) strong white bread flour

1 x 7g sachet of fast-action yeast

1 tsp caster sugar

1 tsp fine sea salt

1½ tbsp olive oil, plus a little extra for serving

1 garlic clove

125g (4oz) mozzarella (check that it's vegetarian)

Approx. 280g (10oz) artichoke hearts in oil

12 pitted Kalamata olives

2 tbsp polenta

150ml (5fl oz) passata

A couple of handfuls of rocket

Preheat the oven to 240°C / 220°C fan / gas mark 9. Place two baking sheets or pizza stones in the oven.

Put the flours, yeast, sugar and salt in a bowl and stir to combine. Make a well in the centre and pour in the oil and roughly 200ml (7fl oz) lukewarm water – enough to make a soft dough. Bring together and knead the dough briefly to form a pliable ball. Cover with the bowl and set aside to rest.

Peel and finely slice the garlic. Tear the mozzarella into pieces. Drain the artichokes and the olives.

Lightly flour the worksurface. Cut the dough in half and roll one half into a circle roughly 20cm (8in) in diameter. Lift the circle onto a large piece of parchment dusted with polenta. Shape and stretch the pizza to reach about 30cm (12in). Ensure that the crust is slightly thicker than the centre of the base. Repeat with the other half of the dough.

Spread the passata over the pizzas and scatter over the artichokes, garlic, olives and mozzarella. Set aside for 10 minutes.

Carefully transfer the pizzas to the baking sheets or pizza stones and bake for 10–12 minutes, until crisp and golden. Serve topped with the rocket and a drizzle of olive oil.

Roasted Broccoli, Caper and Walnut Linguine

This simple pasta makes for an easy lunch or light dinner. The fried walnuts add a creaminess so that the cheese won't be missed if you're keeping it vegan. You want the broccoli to be tender and golden at the edges so be sure to chop the florets small. Use any remaining basil in the Cherry Tomato, Olive and White Wine Spaghetti (see page 87).

SERVES: 4 | VEGETARIAN | PREP TIME: 10 mins | COOKING TIME: 18–20 mins

1 head of broccoli
2 tbsp olive oil
400g (14oz) linguine
1 red chilli
2 garlic cloves
2 tbsp capers
40g (1½oz) walnuts
A small bunch of basil
30g (1¼oz) vegetarian Italian hard cheese (optional)
½ a lemon

Preheat the oven to 220°C / 200°C fan / gas mark 7. Place a large roasting tray on the top shelf of the oven.

Chop the broccoli into small florets. Add to the baking tray in a single layer, season and drizzle over half the oil. Roast for 15 minutes, until tender and singed at the edges.

Meanwhile, cook the linguine in a large pan of water with a generous pinch of salt for roughly 10 minutes, until al dente.

Finely slice the chilli. Peel and crush the garlic. Drain and roughly chop the capers, along with the walnuts. Tear the basil leaves. Grate the cheese, if using.

Heat the remaining oil in a large, non-stick frying pan. Add the chilli, garlic, capers and walnuts and fry gently for 2–3 minutes, until lightly golden. Drain the pasta, reserving a little of the cooking water. Tip the pasta and broccoli into the frying pan, toss to combine and add a little of the cooking water to loosen, if necessary. Season well and add lemon juice to taste. Serve with basil and the cheese, if using.

Creamy Cider Mushrooms on Sourdough with Mustard-dressed Leaves

Wonderfully simple and yet rich and luxurious, these cream and cider mushrooms on toast make a cosy lunch for cold days. Use the largest frying pan that you have and resist the temptation to interfere constantly with the mushrooms; they'll colour much better if they are only turned from time to time.

SERVES: 4 | VEGETARIAN | PREP TIME: 10 mins | COOKING TIME: 15 mins

400g (14oz) chestnut mushrooms
2 garlic cloves
4 sprigs of thyme
1 tbsp Dijon mustard
1 tbsp runny honey
2 tbsp cider vinegar
4 tbsp olive oil plus ½ a tbsp
30g (1¼oz) butter
150ml (5fl oz) dry cider
100ml (3½fl oz) double cream
4 large slices of sourdough bread
100g (3½oz) crisp green salad leaves

Clean and slice the mushrooms. Peel and crush the garlic. Strip the leaves from the thyme.

Make the salad dressing by whisking together the mustard, honey, vinegar and 4 tbsp oil. Season to taste.

Melt the butter in a large frying pan. Add the remaining ½ tbsp oil and, once hot, fry the mushrooms for 4–5 minutes, until deeply browned. Add the garlic and thyme and cook for another minute. Pour in the cider, simmer for 3 minutes, then add the cream and simmer for a final 4–5 minutes, until thickened and glossy. Season to taste.

While the mushrooms are cooking, toast the bread. Dress the leaves and check the seasoning. Spoon the mushrooms over the toast with a generous helping of leaves to the side.

Grilled Mackerel with Rhubarb, Cucumber and Dill

Most commonly cooked into cakes and desserts, rhubarb has a sharp tang when raw that makes a brilliant foil to meat and oily fish. Here it is chopped with cucumber and dill to create a relish to liven up grilled mackerel fillets. Serve with a Scandinavian-inspired new potato salad. Use any remaining dill in the Frying Pan Filo Pie (see page 88).

SERVES: 4 | PREP TIME: 10 mins | COOKING TIME: 20 mins

750g (1lb 10oz) new
   potatoes, scrubbed
1 shallot
1½ tbsp red wine
   vinegar
2 tsp sugar
100g (3½oz) rhubarb
½ a cucumber
A small bunch of dill
A small bunch of
   chives
4 mackerel fillets
1 tbsp Dijon mustard
3 tbsp olive oil

Halve any larger potatoes and keep the small ones whole. Simmer the potatoes in a large pan of boiling water for 15–20 minutes, until just tender to the tip of a knife.

While the potatoes are cooking, peel, halve and finely dice the shallot. Add to a bowl with the vinegar and sugar. Set aside.

Trim the rhubarb and cucumber. Deseed the cucumber and cut both into roughly 0.5cm (¼in) dice. Finely chop the herbs separately. Add the rhubarb, cucumber, half of the dill and a generous pinch of salt to the shallot. Stir to combine.

Preheat the grill to high. Lightly grease a baking tray with some of the oil and lay the mackerel fillets on it, skin side up. Sprinkle the mackerel with salt and grill for 5–6 minutes, until the skin is crisp and the flesh is opaque and flakes easily to the touch.

While the mackerel is cooking, drain the potatoes. Toss with the remaining herbs, mustard and the remaining oil. Season to taste and serve with the mackerel and relish.

Roast Mushroom Gnocchi with Rocket Pesto

Roasting gnocchi renders them golden and crisp on the outside while the inside remains fluffy and tender. Cooking the gnocchi with chestnut mushrooms creates flavour and texture – complemented by a vibrant rocket pesto. There may be more pesto than you need; covered with a layer of oil, it will keep in the fridge for 3 days. Vegan cheeses can be used in place of the nutritional yeast, if preferred.

SERVES: 4 | VEGAN | EQUIPMENT: Blender | PREP TIME: 5–10 mins | COOKING TIME: 20 mins

250g (9oz) chestnut mushrooms

2 x 500g (1lb 2oz) fresh potato gnocchi (check that it's vegan)

4 garlic cloves

4 sprigs of thyme

150ml (5fl oz) olive oil

50g (2oz) hazelnuts

60g (2¼oz) rocket

2 tbsp nutritional yeast

Juice of 1 lemon

Preheat the oven to 220°C / 200°C fan / gas mark 7.

Clean and slice the mushrooms. Tip into a large roasting tin with the gnocchi, 3 cloves of garlic (leave the skins on) and the thyme. Pour over 3 tbsp of the oil and 2 tbsp of water – toss to coat. Season well and roast for 20 minutes, until golden and crisp.

To make the pesto, peel the remaining garlic. Blend with the hazelnuts, rocket, olive oil and nutritional yeast until fairly smooth. Juice the lemon and add to taste. Season well.

Once the gnocchi and mushrooms are cooked, slip the garlic cloves out of their skins, crush with a fork and stir through the gnocchi. Add pesto to taste and serve.

Sea Bass with Leeks and Caper Butter Sauce

Refined and simple, baked bass fillets are served over sweet, soft leeks and finished with a slightly sharp caper and lemon sauce. The bass is quickly roasted to crisp the skin and gently cook the flesh; you'll know it's cooked when it flakes easily to the touch.

SERVES: 4 | PREP TIME: 10 mins | COOKING TIME: 20 mins

2 large leeks
30g (1¼oz) butter
1 lemon
4 sea bass fillets
2 tsp olive oil
4 tbsp capers
200g (7oz) baby
   spinach
60ml (2¼fl oz)
   double cream
2 tsp Dijon mustard

Preheat the oven to 220°C / 200°C fan / gas mark 7.

Trim and finely slice the leeks. Melt half the butter in a large frying pan. Add the leeks and 2 tbsp water and cook gently for about 12–15 minutes, until soft and silky.

Squeeze the juice of the lemon. Pat the bass fillets dry and brush with oil. Place on a foil-lined tray, skin-side up. Sprinkle salt over the skin of the fish and dot over the remaining butter. Drain the capers, add to the tray and bake for 6–8 minutes, until the skin of the fish is crisp and the flesh opaque.

Meanwhile, add spinach in handfuls to the leeks and stir to wilt. Stir through the cream and mustard and season to taste.

Once the fish is cooked, squeeze over half the lemon juice and serve with the leeks. Add more lemon juice and seasoning to taste.

Sardine and Green Olive Spaghetti with Chilli Crumbs

A largely store-cupboard recipe, this robust pasta dish is frugal yet completely delicious. The sardines break up very easily, so add them to the sauce just to warm them through at the end of cooking. Leftover parsley can be used in the Roasted Grape, Goats Cheese and Lentil Salad (see page 47).

SERVES: 4 | PREP TIME: 5–10 mins | COOKING TIME: 20 mins

4 garlic cloves
250g (9oz) cherry
 tomatoes
4 tbsp olive oil
50g (2oz) fresh
 breadcrumbs
Chilli flakes, to taste
300g (10½oz) spaghetti
125g (4oz) pitted
 green olives
 (I like Nocellara),
 chopped
2 tbsp capers, chopped
2 x 125g (4oz) cans
 of sardines in
 tomato sauce
1 lemon, halved
A small bunch of
 parsley, chopped

Bring a large pan of salted water to the boil. Peel and crush the garlic. Halve the cherry tomatoes.

To make the chilli crumbs, heat half the oil in a large frying pan over a low to medium heat. Add the breadcrumbs and fry for 2 minutes, until turning golden. Add half the garlic and add chilli flakes and salt to taste. Cook for a further 1–2 minutes, until fragrant and crisp. Scrape out of the pan and set aside.

Cook the spaghetti for 10–12 minutes, until al dente. Add the remaining oil and garlic to the frying pan and fry over a low to medium heat for 1 minute. Then add the tomatoes and cook for a further 6 min, until beginning to break down.

Drain the pasta, reserving a mugful of the cooking water. Add the olives, capers and sardines to the frying pan – stir gently to warm through. Toss the pasta through the sauce, loosening with a little of the cooking water if necessary.

Check the seasoning and add lemon juice, to taste. Serve the spaghetti with a sprinkling of parsley and breadcrumbs.

Cauliflower Steaks Rarebit

This twist on cauliflower cheese uses a base of nutty, roasted cauliflower 'steaks' for a rich, rarebit sauce. We're using soy sauce instead of the traditional Worcestershire to keep it veggie, plus a generous heap of English mustard for heat and piquancy. The outer parts of the cauliflower will crumble as you slice; these can be roasted and served alongside the steaks. Choose a large cauliflower so that you can get four decent slices out of it. Leftover chives can be used in the Corn and Chorizo Chowder (see page 16).

SERVES: 4 | VEGETARIAN | PREP TIME: 5 mins | COOKING TIME: 20 mins

1 large cauliflower
1½ tbsp olive oil
30g (1¼oz) unsalted
** butter**
30g (1¼oz) plain flour
125ml (4fl oz)
** brown ale**
150g (5oz) mature
** Cheddar cheese**
** (check that it's**
** vegetarian)**
1 tsp English mustard
1 tbsp light soy sauce
A small bunch
** of chives**
Green salad, to serve

Preheat the oven to 220°C / 200°C fan / gas mark 7.

Remove the tough outer leaves from the cauliflower and cut into 'steaks' roughly 2cm (¾in) thick. Brush with the oil, season to taste and roast on a baking tray for 12–15 minutes, until golden and just tender.

Meanwhile, melt the butter in a small saucepan. Once foaming, add the flour and cook, stirring, for 1–2 minutes, until biscuity-smelling. Remove from the heat and gradually whisk in the ale. Grate the cheese and add to the pan with the mustard and soy sauce. Season to taste. Finely chop the chives.

Preheat the grill to high. Once the cauliflower has roasted, spoon the rarebit sauce over the steaks and grill for 2–3 minutes, until golden and bubbling. Sprinkle with the chives and serve with a crunchy, green salad.

One Pots & Traybakes

Braised Chicken with Radishes and Peas

This light, fresh stew celebrates some of the best flavours of spring. Be gentle when cooking the chicken – too high a heat and it will be tough, but a low simmer for 20 minutes will ensure that it is just cooked through and tender. Leftover tarragon can be used in the Lamb Chops with Mustard and Tarragon Potatoes (see page 106).

SERVES: 4 | PREP TIME: 5 mins | COOKING TIME: 30–35 mins

A bunch of spring
    onions
4 garlic cloves
2 tbsp olive oil
500g (1lb 2oz) skinless
    chicken thigh fillets
100ml (3½fl oz) dry
    white wine
500ml (17fl oz) chicken
    stock
6 stalks of tarragon
200g (7oz) radishes
A small bunch
    of parsley
1 lemon
200g (7oz) frozen
    petits pois
1 tbsp Dijon mustard
Crusty bread, to serve

Separate the white and the green parts of the spring onions. Cut the white ends into 2cm (¾in) pieces and finely slice the green parts. Peel and crush the garlic.

Heat the oil in a large, high-sided frying or sauté pan. Pat the chicken dry and season well. Add to the pan and fry for 4–5 minutes, turning from time to time, until golden. Add the white parts of the spring onion and the garlic and fry for a further 2 minutes.

Pour in the wine. Once bubbling, add the stock and 4 of the tarragon stalks, and simmer gently for 20 minutes, until the chicken is tender and just cooked through.

Cut the radishes in half and add to the pan for the last 10 minutes of cooking. Finely chop the remaining tarragon. Finely chop the parsley. Slice the lemon in half.

Add the peas and mustard to the stew and simmer for 2–3 minutes, until just tender. Season and add lemon juice to taste. Scatter over the green parts of the spring onion and the chopped herbs to finish. Serve with crusty bread.

Courgette, Artichoke and Feta Tart

Sharp, salty feta can be a little overpowering. By combining with crème fraîche, the cheese is lightened to make a base for a simple-to-prepare tart. There's no need to beat the mixture until completely smooth: you just want it to be well combined, creamy and spreadable. You only need a couple of sprigs of mint in this recipe; use the remainder in the Halloumi, Watermelon and Sumac Salad (see page 45).

SERVES: 4 | VEGETARIAN | PREP TIME: 10 mins | COOKING TIME: 20 mins

320g (approx. 11oz) ready-rolled puff pastry sheet

100g (3½oz) feta (check that it's vegetarian)

75g (3oz) crème fraîche

1 medium courgette

175g (6oz) marinated artichokes in oil

2 sprigs of mint

Preheat the oven to 220°C / 200°C fan / gas mark 7. Place a baking sheet on the top shelf of the oven. Unroll the puff pastry onto another baking sheet lined with parchment. Use a sharp knife to score a 1.5cm (½in) border around the edges, taking care not to cut all the way through. Set aside in the fridge.

Put the feta in a mixing bowl with the crème fraîche and mash with a fork to create a spreadable, creamy mixture. Season well with pepper.

Slice the courgette into ribbons using a vegetable peeler, working your way around the courgette until you reach the seedy core (this can be used in soups or stews). Wring out any excess liquid using a clean tea towel or kitchen roll.

Spread the feta mixture over the pastry, keeping clear of the borders. Drain the artichokes, reserving 1 tbsp of the oil. Arrange over the tart with the courgettes and drizzle with the reserved oil.

Carefully slide the parchment onto the hot baking sheet and bake for 16–20 minutes, until the pastry is well risen and golden. Pick the mint leaves and roughly tear. Sprinkle over the tart and serve.

Baked Cod with Fennel and Tomatoes

Inspired by Mediterranean flavours, these simple ingredients are all cooked together in one tin for maximum flavour and minimal effort. Check that the cod is cooked by pressing the flesh gently – it will flake easily to the touch when ready. Serve with chunks of crusty bread to mop up the juices. Leftover parsley can be used in the Caponata Traybake (see page 91).

SERVES: 4 | PREP TIME: 10 mins | COOKING TIME: 25–30 mins

A pinch of saffron
1 fennel bulb
1 shallot
200g (7oz) cherry
   tomatoes
2½ tbsp olive oil
2 large garlic cloves
2 x 400g (14oz) cans
   cannellini beans
16 pitted Kalamata
   olives
1 tbsp tomato purée
2 x 400g (14oz) cans
   chopped tomatoes
A pinch of sugar
½ a lemon
A handful of parsley
4 cod loin fillets
Crusty bread, to serve

Preheat the oven to 200°C / 180°C fan / gas mark 6.

Mix the saffron with 1 tbsp boiling water and set aside.

Trim and finely slice the fennel, reserving the fronds. Peel and finely slice the shallot. Tip the fennel and shallot into a roasting tin with the cherry tomatoes and 2 tbsp of the oil. Season to taste and roast for 10 minutes, until the fennel has softened slightly.

While the fennel is cooking, peel and crush the garlic. Drain and rinse the beans and halve the olives. Add the garlic, tomato purée, chopped tomatoes, a pinch of sugar, the beans, olives and saffron water to the tin. Stir gently and return to the oven for a further 5 minutes.

Finely zest and juice the lemon half. Roughly chop the parsley. Add the cod fillets to the pan, pour over the remaining oil and season. Return to the oven for a further 10–12 minutes, until the cod flakes gently to the touch.

Sprinkle over the lemon zest, juice and parsley. Serve with crusty bread.

Oregano Lamb and Pistachio Traybake

Garlic, lemon and oregano-scented lamb leg steaks are quickly roasted over Mediterranean vegetables and slices of potatoes, allowing for the flavours to blend and percolate. Finish with bright oregano and sweet, creamy pistachios. These timings are for pink lamb; adjust according to your preference.

SERVES: 4 | PREP TIME: 10 mins | COOKING TIME: 30 mins

1 lemon

2 tsp dried oregano

4 tbsp olive oil

500g (1lb 2oz) new
  potatoes

4 garlic cloves

4 lamb leg steaks

2 courgettes

500g (1lb 2oz) cherry
  tomatoes

2 sprigs fresh oregano

40g (1½oz) pistachios

Preheat the oven to 220°C / 200°C fan / gas mark 7. Place a large roasting tray on the top shelf of the oven.

Finely zest and juice the lemon. Mix with the oregano and oil and season well. Cut the potatoes into slices 0.5cm (¼in) thick and tip into a bowl. Pour over half the oil and lemon mix and toss until the potatoes are well coated. Spread out in a single layer on the baking tray and roast for 10 minutes.

Meanwhile, peel and crush the garlic. Add the lamb steaks to the empty bowl, along with the garlic and remaining oil mixture. Turn the lamb to coat.

Trim and roughly slice the courgettes. Add to the bowl along with the cherry tomatoes and fresh oregano. Season again, if liked.

After 10 minutes, spread the vegetables out onto to the tray and pop the lamb steaks on top. Roast for a further 20 minutes, until the vegetables are tender, and the lamb is well coloured and pink within. Roughly chop the pistachios and sprinkle over the top to finish.

Bean and Dill Pilaf
with Green Tahini

Inspired by a traditional Persian rice dish, this simple pilaf is studded with beans and served with garlic, dill and a lemon and herb tahini. The rice needs to be rinsed really well to remove the starch – this will ensure fluffy, well-separated grains. To make the dish vegan, omit the butter and use 3 tbsp of oil.

SERVES: 4 | **VEGETARIAN** | **EQUIPMENT:** Blender | **PREP TIME:** 10 mins | **COOKING TIME:** 20–25 mins

1 onion
1 tbsp olive oil
25g (1oz) butter
250g (9oz) white
   basmati rice
2 garlic cloves
500ml (17fl oz) hot
   vegetable stock
125g (4oz) runner
   beans
125g (4oz) fine green
   beans
100g (3½oz) edamame
   beans
A small bunch of dill
1 lemon
75g (3oz) tahini
1 small bunch parsley
1 small bunch mint

Peel and finely chop the onion. Heat the oil and butter in a large, lidded saucepan. Once foaming, add the onion and cook gently for 5–6 minutes, until softened.

Rinse the rice in a sieve and tip into a bowl. Cover with water and set aside for a few minutes. Peel and crush the garlic. Add to the pan and cook for 1 minute, until fragrant. Drain the rice and stir into the onion mixture. Pour over the hot stock, bring up to the boil, cover and simmer very gently for 8 minutes.

Trim the runner beans, remove the string with a vegetable peeler and cut into 2cm (¾in) lengths. Trim the green beans and cut to the same length as the runners. Once the rice has cooked for 10 minutes, add all the vegetables to the pan, quickly re-cover and cook for a further 5 minutes, until the beans and the rice are tender.

Meanwhile, roughly chop the dill and set half aside. Squeeze the lemon and add half the juice, the tahini, the remaining herbs and 4 tbsp of water to a blender. Blitz briefly until the herbs are finely chopped.

Fluff the rice with a fork and season to taste. Serve with the chopped dill, the tahini and more lemon juice, if liked.

Cherry Tomato, Olive and White Wine Spaghetti

This lazy yet delicious spaghetti throws out the rulebook as everything is cooked together in one pan. The spaghetti cooks to al dente, absorbing the flavours of the wine, olives, capers and tomatoes as it cooks. The only essential is using a pan wide enough for the pasta. Leftover herbs can be used in the Corn and Courgette Salad with a Smoky Tomato Dressing (see page 35).

SERVES: 4 | VEGAN | PREP TIME: 15 mins | COOKING TIME: 8–10 mins

1 shallot, peeled and
  thinly sliced
2 garlic cloves, peeled
  and crushed
50g (2oz) Kalamata
  olives, halved
2 tbsp capers, drained
  and roughly chopped
400g (14oz) cherry
  tomatoes
100ml (3½fl oz)
  vegan white wine
60ml (2¼fl oz) olive oil
400g (14oz) spaghetti
A small bunch
  of parsley
A small bunch of basil

Put the chopped shallot, garlic, olives and capers into a wide pan or flameproof casserole dish. Add the tomatoes, white wine, olive oil and spaghetti and pour over with 900ml (2 pints) boiling water. Cover and bring to a boil. Remove the lid and cook for 8–10 minutes, tossing with tongs regularly, until the pasta is just tender and the water has almost been absorbed.

While the pasta is cooking, roughly chop the parsley and tear the basil leaves. Serve with the pasta.

Frying Pan Filo Pie

This simplified version of the Greek spinach and feta pie, Spanakopita, is enriched with pine nuts and ricotta and bound with eggs to help the pie set: it will be on the table within 40 minutes.

SERVES: 4 | VEGETARIAN | EQUIPMENT: Hob-to-oven pan | PREP TIME: 20 mins | COOKING TIME: 25 mins

4 spring onions
2 garlic cloves
400g (14oz) young
   spinach
50g (2oz) pine nuts
2 tbsp olive oil, plus
   extra for brushing
A small bunch of dill
4 large eggs
100g (3½oz) ricotta
200g (7oz) feta (make
   sure it's vegetarian)
A pinch of nutmeg
5 sheets filo pastry

Preheat the oven to 200°C / 180°C fan / gas mark 6. Place a baking sheet on the top shelf of the oven.

Trim and finely slice the spring onions. Peel and crush the garlic. Tip the spinach into a colander and pour over boiling water to wilt. Leave to cool and drain.

Toast the pine nuts in a medium to large oven-proof frying pan approx. 22cm (8½in) wide. Once lightly golden, add 1 tbsp of oil, followed by the spring onions and garlic. Cook gently for 2–3 minutes, until beginning to soften.

Finely chop the dill and put in a mixing bowl with the eggs and ricotta. Beat until fairly smooth, then crumble in the feta and stir through a pinch of nutmeg. Squeeze the spinach to release any excess water. Add to the bowl with the pine-nut mixture and stir to combine. Season carefully.

Wipe out the pan and brush with oil. Working quickly, lay a sheet of the filo out on your work surface and brush liberally with oil. Top with another sheet of pastry and repeat until you have 4 layers. Line the pan with the pastry, letting it hang over the edges. Pour in the filling and fold the overhanging pastry over the top. Scrunch the final sheet of pastry on top, brush with a little more oil, and bake on the pre-heated tray for 18–20 minutes, until crisp and golden. Leave for a few minutes before cutting into slices to serve.

Red Pepper and Butter Bean Eggs

Sweet, tangy and infinitely versatile, roasted peppers from jars are a fantastic shortcut ingredient to have on standby. Here they are cooked down with butter beans in a smoky tomato sauce and finished with eggs. You will need a large frying pan in order to accommodate enough eggs to feed four people well.

SERVES: 4 | VEGETARIAN | PREP TIME: 5 mins | COOKING TIME: 25 mins

2 tbsp olive oil

1 red onion, peeled and finely sliced

2 garlic cloves

1 x 400g (14oz) can butter beans

4 red peppers from a jar

2½ tsp smoked paprika

2 tsp dried oregano

2 tbsp tomato purée

1 x 400g (14oz) can chopped tomatoes

80g (3¼oz) baby spinach

8 very fresh medium eggs

100g (3½oz) feta (make sure it's vegetarian), optional

Heat the oil in a large frying pan or casserole dish. Add the onion and cook for 5 minutes, until softened.

While the onion is cooking, peel and crush the garlic. Drain the butter beans and rinse in a sieve. Drain the peppers and roughly slice.

Add the garlic, paprika and oregano to the pan. Cook for 1 minute, then add the tomato purée, chopped tomatoes and half a can of water. Stir in the butter beans and red peppers and simmer gently for 6–8 minutes, until slightly reduced. Add the spinach in handfuls, stir through and cook for 1–2 minutes to wilt.

Season the sauce to taste and make 8 indentations with a spoon. Crack an egg into each, cover with a lid or foil and simmer for a further 6–8 minutes, until the egg whites are set and the yolks are still slightly runny.

Season to taste and crumble over the feta, if using, to finish.

Caponata Traybake

Sicilian caponata – a sweet, savoury stew with a subtle background tang of vinegar – is traditionally cooked slowly over a gentle heat. To speed things up, this recipe comprises traditional caponata ingredients but lets the oven do the work in a fraction of the time. Keep an eye on the vegetables as they roast; any burnt bits will taste bitter. Any remaining parsley can be used in the Roasted Chickpeas and Cauliflower on Garlic and Mint Yogurt (see page 95).

SERVES: 4 | VEGAN | PREP TIME: 10 mins | COOKING TIME: 30 mins

1 large red onion

2 aubergines

2 sticks of celery

2 peppers (different colours)

250g (9oz) cherry tomatoes

4 garlic cloves

2 tbsp raisins or sultanas

2 tbsp capers

75ml (3fl oz) olive oil

40g (1½oz) pine nuts

2 tbsp balsamic vinegar

A small bunch of parsley

Preheat the oven to 220°C / 200°C fan / gas mark 7. Place a large roasting tin in the oven to warm.

Peel, halve and slice the onion into slim wedges. Trim and cut the aubergines into 2cm (¾in) chunks. Trim and finely slice the celery. Trim, deseed and slice the peppers quite finely.

Tip the chopped vegetables, cherry tomatoes, whole garlic cloves and raisins or sultanas into a large mixing bowl. Drain the capers and add to the bowl along with half the oil. Season well, toss to combine and spread out into the roasting tin in a single layer. Roast for 30 minutes, adding the pine nuts for the final 5 minutes.

Meanwhile, mix the remaining oil with the balsamic vinegar. Roughly chop the parsley.

Once the vegetables are tender and well coloured, pour over the dressing, check the seasoning and serve sprinkled with parsley.

Prawn and Saffron Rice with Roasted Peppers

The flavours of a paella in simplified, speedy form. This dish is by no means authentic but delicious nonetheless. Soaking the rice prior to cooking removes the starch and speeds up the cooking time slightly. Use any leftover parsley in the Baked Cod with Fennel and Tomatoes (see page 82).

SERVES: 4 | PREP TIME: 5 mins | COOKING TIME: 25 mins

2 shallots

2 tbsp olive oil

300g (10½oz) basmati rice

A pinch of saffron

2 garlic cloves

2 large ripe tomatoes

200g (7oz) roasted peppers from a jar

2 tsp smoked paprika

600ml (1 pint) chicken or fish stock

A small handful of parsley

1 lemon

300g (10½oz) raw king prawns

200g (7oz) frozen peas

Peel and finely slice the shallots. Heat the oil in a large sauté pan with a lid. Add the shallots, cover and cook gently for 4–5 minutes, until beginning to soften.

Rinse the rice well and tip into a bowl. Cover with cold water and set aside. Mix the saffron in a small bowl with 1 tbsp boiling water.

Peel and crush the garlic. Roughly chop the tomatoes. Drain and slice the peppers. Add the garlic and paprika to the shallots and cook for 1 minute. Drain the rice. Stir the paprika, tomatoes, peppers and rice into the pan and pour over the stock. Bring up to the boil, cover and simmer over a low heat for 14 minutes, until the rice is just tender.

Roughly chop the parsley and cut the lemon into wedges. Add the prawns to the pan for the final 5 minutes of cooking time and the peas for the final 2 minutes. Stir the peas and prawns through the rice. Serve with parsley and a wedge of lemon.

Butternut, Sage and Hazelnut Orzotto

Substituting risotto rice with orzo is a clever shortcut for a riff on a classic and comforting dish. Cooked in much the same way as a risotto but taking a fraction of the time, the orzo in this recipe is cooked with leeks, sweet butternut squash, wine and stock. Finish with crisp sage and hazelnuts and vegetarian or vegan hard cheese. Use the remaining sage in the Squash and Chestnut Soup (see page 25).

SERVES: 4 | VEGETARIAN (OR VEGAN) | PREP TIME: 5 mins | COOKING TIME: 25 mins

1 leek

2 tbsp olive oil

½ a butternut squash (about 600g/1¼lb)

2 garlic cloves, peeled and crushed

100ml (3½fl oz) dry white wine (make sure it's vegetarian or vegan)

300g (10½oz) orzo

1 litre (1¾ pints) vegetable stock

50g (2oz) hazelnuts

8 sage leaves

40g (1½oz) vegetarian (or vegan) Italian hard cheese

Trim and finely slice the leek. Heat 1½ tbsp of the oil in a large saucepan and cook the leek gently for 8 minutes, until softened.

Meanwhile, peel, deseed and chop half the squash into 1cm (⅜in) cubes. Coarsely grate the rest.

Add the garlic to the leek and cook for 1 minute. Add the wine and, once bubbling, stir in the squash and orzo, along with half the stock. Bring up to a simmer and allow to bubble away, stirring from time to time. Add more stock by the ladleful as the orzo absorbs it. Continue until the squash and orzo are just tender – about 10–12 minutes.

While the orzotto is cooking, roughly chop the hazelnuts. Heat the remaining oil in a frying pan and add the hazelnuts and sage leaves. Fry for 3–4 minutes until the hazelnuts are golden and the sage is crisp. Grate the cheese.

To finish, stir half the cheese into the orzotto and season to taste. Sprinkle over the hazelnuts, sage and the remaining cheese to serve.

Roasted Chickpeas and Cauliflower on Garlic and Mint Yogurt

Gently spiced, nutty cauliflower is tempered with cool, mint-flecked yogurt. The combination of hot roasted vegetables over the yogurt makes a wonderful contrast but the dish can also be eaten at room temperature. You can use any remaining mint in the Halloumi, Watermelon and Sumac Salad (see page 45).

SERVES: 4 | VEGETARIAN | PREP TIME: 10 mins | COOKING TIME: 20 mins

1 cauliflower
1 red onion
2 x 400g (14oz) cans
   chickpeas
3 tbsp olive oil
1 lemon
2 garlic cloves
A small bunch of mint
A small bunch
   of parsley
1½ tbsp medium
   curry powder
4 tbsp mixed seeds
250g (9oz) thick
   Greek yogurt
80g (3¼oz) baby
   spinach

Preheat the oven to 220°C / 200°C fan / gas mark 7.

Cut the cauliflower into small florets, reserving any smaller leaves. Peel and slice the onion into thin wedges. Drain the chickpeas and rinse well. Tip the chickpeas into a bowl and toss with the vegetables and oil. Season well, spread out over two baking trays and bake for 10 minutes.

Meanwhile, zest the lemon and cut into wedges. Peel and crush the garlic. Shred the mint leaves and roughly chop the parsley.

After 10 minutes, sprinkle the curry powder and seeds over the vegetables and stir to coat. Return to the oven for a further 8–10 minutes until the vegetables are golden and just tender and the chickpeas are crisp.

Meanwhile, mix the yogurt with the lemon zest and mint. Season to taste. Spoon the yogurt into a serving dish and top with the spinach, roasted vegetables and parsley. Serve with lemon wedges.

Baked Figs and Feta with Honey and Walnuts

Sweet, yielding figs are the perfect foil for sharp and salty feta in this bake. Top with walnuts and sherry vinegar and scoop up to eat with chunks of crusty bread. Serve with peppery rocket, for balance. Any leftover thyme can be used in the Veggie Sausage and Kale Bake With Cheesy Polenta (see page 122).

SERVES: 4 | VEGETARIAN | PREP TIME: 10 mins | COOKING TIME: 18–20 mins

1 shallot

8 ripe figs

2 x 200g (7oz) packs of feta (make sure it's vegetarian)

6 sprigs thyme

30g (1½oz) walnuts

1½ tbsp honey

4 tbsp olive oil

3 tbsp sherry vinegar

80g (3¼oz) rocket

Crusty bread, to serve

Preheat the oven to 200°C / 180°C fan / gas mark 6.

Peel, halve and finely slice the shallot. Halve the figs and arrange in a single layer on a baking tray. Nestle the blocks of feta among the figs. Roughly strip the leaves from the thyme and break up the walnuts with your fingertips. Sprinkle both over the feta and figs and drizzle over the honey, olive oil and vinegar.

Season with pepper and bake for 18–20 minutes, until the figs are sticky and soft and the feta is just lightly golden.

Leave to cool for a few minutes and serve with rocket and crusty bread to mop up the juices.

Chicken and Focaccia Bake with Rosemary Butter

This all-in-one meal is a riot of flavour and texture; crisp focaccia, bright cavolo nero and tender chicken give way to a rich, creamy sauce. You'll need to use a large roasting tin to give everything enough room to cook well in the time. Skin-on chicken breasts will ensure that the meat doesn't dry out, so do try to seek them out.

SERVES: 4 | **PREP TIME: 10 mins** | **COOKING TIME: 20–25 mins**

2 shallots

1 garlic bulb

1 lemon

4 sprigs of rosemary

30g (1¼oz) butter, softened

4 skin-on chicken breasts

2 tbsp olive oil

125ml (4fl oz) dry white wine

200g (7oz) cavolo nero

200–300g (7–10½oz) focaccia

100g (3½oz) crème fraîche

1 tsp English mustard

Preheat the oven to 200°C / 180°C fan / gas mark 6.

Halve and peel the shallots. Cut into quarters. Slice the garlic bulb in half horizontally. Cut the lemon into quarters.

Finely chop the rosemary and mix with the butter. Season to taste.

Arrange the shallots, garlic and lemon in a large, shallow roasting tin and nestle the chicken breasts among them. Drizzle over half the oil and dot the butter evenly over everything. Pour the wine into t he tin and bake for 15 minutes.

While the chicken is cooking, shred the cavolo nero. Tear the focaccia into chunks.

Mix together the crème fraîche and mustard. Stir into the tin and then add the cavolo nero and focaccia. Drizzle over the remaining oil and continue to bake for a further 5–10 minutes, until the chicken is completely cooked through.

Spring Greens and Spiced Tomato Dal

Soothing and creamy, this dal is spiced delicately enough to be popular with all the family. If you're cooking for very young children, hold back on the green chilli and salt. The lentils have a habit of sticking to the pan; regular stirring with a whisk will keep them moving and help them to break down. Although the dal will be delicious eaten straight away, it's even better reheated the following day. Any leftover coriander can be used in the Black Bean and Tomato Chipotle Soup (see page 19).

SERVES: 4 | VEGAN | PREP TIME: 5 mins | COOKING TIME: 25–30 mins

250g (9oz) red lentils

400ml (14fl oz) can
  coconut milk

1 onion

2 tbsp coconut oil

2cm (¾in) piece
  of ginger

400g (14oz) tomatoes

1 tsp black mustard
  seeds

2 tsp ground cumin

1½ tsp ground
  coriander

1 green chilli

200g (7oz) spring
  greens

A handful of coriander

Rinse the lentils well in a sieve. Tip into a pan. Add the coconut milk (saving 1 tbsp for serving), along with 500ml (17fl oz) of water. Bring to the boil and simmer for 20 minutes, stirring every so often with a whisk, until tender and creamy.

While the lentils are cooking, halve, peel and finely chop the onion. Heat the oil in a large frying pan and gently fry the onion for 8–10 minutes, until softened. Peel and finely grate the ginger. Roughly dice the tomatoes. Add the spices and ginger to the frying pan and cook for 1 minute, then add the tomatoes and 2 tbsp of water. Simmer for 5–6 minutes, until the tomatoes are starting to break down. Finely slice the green chilli. Shred the spring greens. Roughly chop the coriander.

Add the spring greens to the frying pan in handfuls. Cook for 1 minute, until beginning to wilt, then pour in the lentils. Give everything a good stir and season to taste. Stir through the reserved coconut milk. Serve in bowls topped with the sliced chilli and coriander.

Feasts

Crab Tostadas with Pea Guacamole and Pickled Shallots

Fried, toasted or oven-baked tortillas provide a crisp base for myriad tostada toppings. This recipe combines avocado with peas to make a sweeter guacamole for the delicate crab to nestle into. I've suggested using white crab meat for its delicate flavour but you could use a mix of white and brown. Use any leftover coriander in the Spring Greens and Spiced Tomato Dal (see page 100).

SERVES: 4 | **EQUIPMENT:** Pestle and mortar or blender | **PREP TIME:** 20 mins | **COOKING TIME:** 6–8 mins

12 mini tortillas
2 tbsp olive oil
150g (5oz) frozen peas
1 garlic clove
4 spring onions
1 red chilli
1 small bunch
  of coriander
2 limes
2 ripe avocados
4 tbsp soured cream
100g (3½oz) white
  crab meat
Hot sauce, to serve

Preheat the oven to 200°C / 180°C fan / gas mark 6.

Brush the tortillas with the olive oil and divide between two baking sheets in a single layer. Bake for 6–8 minutes, until crisp.

Cover the peas with boiling water and set aside for a few minutes to defrost. Peel the garlic. Trim and finely slice the spring onions. Slice the chilli and roughly chop the coriander. Slice the limes in half. Drain the peas.

Halve and de-stone the avocados. Scoop out the flesh and combine with the drained peas, the garlic, half the spring onions and the juice of one of the limes. Season and blend until fairly smooth.

Spread the guacamole out over the tortillas and top with the soured cream and crab meat. Sprinkle with the coriander and hot sauce and add a drizzle of lime juice, to taste.

Lamb Chops with Mustard and Tarragon Potatoes

As it is so rich in flavour, lamb is often at its best when prepared very simply. In this recipe, lamb chops are marinated briefly in garlic, olive oil and red wine vinegar and served with potatoes tossed with mustard and slightly anise-flavoured tarragon. If the weather calls for it, the lamb can be barbecued instead of grilled. Any leftover tarragon can be used in the Herby Chard and Gruyère Frittata (see page 58).

SERVES: 4 | PREP TIME: 10 mins | COOKING TIME: 20 mins

2 garlic cloves

3 tbsp olive oil

2 tbsp red wine vinegar

8 lamb chops

1kg (2lb 3oz) new potatoes

1 echalion shallot

1 tbsp Dijon mustard

A small bunch of tarragon

80g (3¼oz) watercress, to serve

Peel and crush the garlic. Combine with 1 tbsp of the oil and half the vinegar. Pour over the lamb chops, season well and set aside briefly.

Halve the new potatoes and cut any large ones into quarters, so they are all roughly the same size. Boil in salted water for 16–18 minutes, until tender to the tip of a knife.

Preheat the grill to high. While the potatoes are cooking, peel and finely chop the shallot and combine with the remaining vinegar and oil and the mustard. Finely chop the tarragon.

Remove the lamb from the marinade and pat dry. Grill for 3–4 minutes each side for pink, or until cooked to your liking.

Drain the potatoes and toss with the shallot, tarragon and mustard. Season to taste and serve with the watercress.

Chorizo, Sweetheart Cabbage and New Potato Stew

A hearty and warming stew, perfect for cooler summer evenings. Sweetheart or hispi cabbages are available through the summer and early autumn and favoured for their mellow, sweet flavour. Substitute with savoy cabbage during the winter months.

SERVES: 4 | **PREP TIME:** 5 mins | **COOKING TIME:** 25 mins

250g (9oz) cooking
   chorizo
1 tbsp olive oil
1 onion
2 garlic cloves
500g (1lb 2oz)
   new potatoes
A pinch of saffron
1 litre (1¾ pints)
   chicken stock
2 tsp smoked paprika
1 tsp dried thyme
2 tbsp tomato purée
2 x 400g (14oz) cans
   chopped tomatoes
1 sweetheart cabbage
A small bunch
   of parsley

Cut the chorizo into slices 1cm (⅜in) thick. Pour the oil into a large saucepan and add the chorizo. Place over a medium heat and fry for 2–3 minutes, until the fat has started to render.

Meanwhile, peel, halve and finely slice the onion. Add to the pan and cook gently for 5 minutes until softened.

While the onion is cooking, peel and crush the garlic. Cut the potatoes into slices 1cm (⅜in) thick. Crumble the saffron into the stock. Add the garlic, paprika, thyme and tomato purée to the pan; cook for 1 minute and then add the potatoes, tomatoes and stock. Simmer for 10 minutes, until the potatoes are almost tender.

Meanwhile, strip the cabbage of any tough outer leaves. Halve, cut out the tough core and finely shred. Finely chop the parsley.

Add the cabbage to the stew and simmer for a final 5 minutes. Season to taste and serve sprinkled with the parsley.

Roasted Togarashi Salmon with Citrus Sesame Dressing

Japanese shichimi togarashi is a mix of seven spices comprising chillies, aromatics, nori and seeds. It lends heat and umami to a variety of dishes and is a great way of adding flavour in a dash. You'll find it in most supermarkets; it varies in heat so adjust the amount used according to your spice preference.

SERVES: 4 | **PREP TIME:** 10 mins | **COOKING TIME:** 30 mins

250g (9oz) brown rice (I like basmati)

200g (7oz) frozen edamame beans

1 head of broccoli

1 tbsp sunflower oil

2cm (¾in) piece of ginger

4 spring onions

4 salmon fillets

1 tbsp toasted sesame oil

3 tbsp light soy or tamari

2 tsp shichimi togarashi

4 tbsp tahini

Juice of 1 lime

1½ tsp mirin

A pinch of sugar

Preheat the oven to 200°C / 180°C fan / gas mark 6.

Rinse the rice in a sieve and add to a pan with 500ml (17fl oz) water. Bring to a boil and simmer for 25 minutes, adding the edamame beans for the final 5 minutes. Cover and leave to stand.

Cut the broccoli into small florets and the stalk into slices 1cm (⅜in) thick. Tip into a large roasting tin, toss with the sunflower oil and roast for 5 minutes.

Peel and finely grate the ginger. Finely slice the spring onions. Fold the ginger and half of the spring onions through the broccoli and make four spaces for the salmon fillets. Sprinkle over the sesame oil, 2 tbsp of the soy and the togarashi and return to the oven for 10–12 minutes, until the salmon is just cooked through (it will flake easily to the touch when ready).

To make the dressing, combine the tahini, lime juice, mirin and sugar.

Drain the rice, if necessary, and top with the salmon and vegetables. Drizzle over the dressing and sprinkle over the remaining spring onions before serving.

Sesame Beef and Quick Pickle Wraps

Wrapping tender sesame beef, noodles and quickly pickled vegetables in lettuce leaves adds fantastic texture and freshness. There are quite a few ingredients in this recipe, but they all come together in 30 minutes. The instructions below are for a medium-rare steak. Add a further minute for medium and 2 minutes for well done.

SERVES: 4 | PREP TIME: 20 mins | COOKING TIME: 10 mins

500g (1lb 2oz) sirloin
   or rump steak
3 tbsp light soy sauce
3 tbsp soft light
   brown sugar
4 tbsp rice vinegar
¼ tsp salt
A pinch of chilli flakes
2 medium carrots
1 medium cucumber
2 cloves of garlic
4 spring onions
1 tbsp sunflower or
   groundnut oil
1 tbsp toasted
   sesame oil
2 tsp sesame seeds
100g (3½oz) fine
   vermicelli rice
   noodles
1 round lettuce

Put the steak in a non-metallic bowl and pour over 1 tbsp of the soy sauce. Set aside for now.

In a large bowl, mix 2 tbsp of the sugar, the rice vinegar, salt and chilli flakes. Peel the carrots. Using a vegetable peeler, slice the carrots and cucumber into ribbons. Stop when you reach the seeds of the cucumber. Add to the bowl and toss to coat in the pickling liquor.

Peel and crush the garlic. Trim and chop the spring onions into pieces 2cm (¾in) long.

Heat the sunflower oil in a large frying pan or wok. Add the steak and fry for 2 minutes each side for medium-rare. Add the garlic, spring onions, remaining soy sauce, remaining sugar, sesame oil and sesame seeds and stir-fry for a further 1–2 minutes, until fragrant. Remove from the pan and rest for 5 minutes.

While the steak is resting, sit the noodles in boiled water for 5 minutes, until just tender. Drain into a sieve.

Separate the lettuce leaves. Slice the steak. Divide the pickles and noodles between the lettuce leaves, top with the steak and serve. Eat rolled up into wraps.

Whole Grilled Aubergines with Garlic and Tahini Sauce

Grilling or barbecuing whole aubergines renders the flesh smoky and sweet in a short amount of time. Once grilled, the flesh is served with a garlic, maple and tahini sauce, a crisp green salad and pittas. An easy mezze in minutes.

SERVES: 4 | VEGETARIAN | PREP TIME: 5–10 mins | COOKING TIME: 20–25 mins

4 medium aubergines

Olive oil, for brushing

2 garlic cloves

1 lemon

4 pickled chillies (optional)

2 little gem lettuces

A small bunch of parsley

A small bunch of mint

75g (3oz) pitted green olives (I like Nocellara)

4 tbsp tahini

½ tbsp maple syrup

1–2 tsp hot sauce (to your liking)

4 pitta breads

Preheat the grill or barbecue to high. Once hot, pierce each aubergine with a knife and brush with a little olive oil. Grill or barbecue for 20–25 minutes, turning occasionally, until the skin is charred and the flesh is tender within.

While the aubergine is cooking, peel and crush the garlic. Juice the lemon. Slice the chillies, if using. Separate the leaves of the little gem and plunge into ice-cold water. Pick the leaves from the herbs and add to the water. Finely chop the parsley stalks. Halve the pitted olives.

To make the dressing, mix the garlic, tahini, maple syrup and hot sauce together. Add half the lemon juice and 1–2 tbsp water, until pourable. Check the seasoning and add more lemon juice and / or hot sauce, to your liking. Finally, stir in the chopped parsley stalks.

Toast the pittas under the grill or on the barbecue. Drain the salad well and add the olives. To serve, cut open the aubergines and scoop out the smoky flesh. Serve with the salad, pittas and plenty of the dressing.

Sweet Roasted Veg with Nigella-seed Flatbreads and Paprika Yogurt

This recipe has a few elements to it but while the oven does the heavy lifting with the vegetables, you can get on with making the flatbreads and paprika yogurt.

SERVES: 4 | VEGETARIAN | PREP TIME: 10 mins | COOKING TIME: 30 mins

1 red onion, peeled and cut into thin wedges

2 red peppers, deseeded and roughly sliced

1 aubergine, cut into slices 1.5cm (½in) thick

500g (1lb 2oz) whole cherry tomatoes

1 x 400g (14oz) can chickpeas

1½ tsp cumin seeds

4 tbsp olive oil, plus extra for frying

4 sprigs of thyme

4 whole garlic cloves

250g (9oz) self-raising flour

500g (1lb 2oz) Greek yogurt

1½ tsp nigella seeds

2 tsp smoked paprika

1 tbsp pomegranate molasses

Preheat the oven to 220°C / 200°C fan / gas mark 7. Place a large roasting tin on the top shelf of the oven.

Tip the vegetables and tomatoes into a large mixing bowl. Drain the chickpeas and add to the bowl with the cumin seeds, 3 tbsp of the oil, thyme and garlic. Season well, toss and spread evenly in the roasting tin. Roast for 25–30 minutes, turning halfway, until just tender.

Meanwhile, sift the flour into the empty mixing bowl. Make a well in the centre and spoon in half the yogurt, the nigella seeds and ½ tsp salt. Bring together with a wooden spoon to form a soft dough. Divide into 4 and roll out on a lightly floured surface into ovals, about 0.5cm (¼in) thick.

Heat a large frying pan over a high heat. Brush the pan with a little of the remaining oil and add two flatbreads. Cook for 2–3 minutes each side, until well coloured and risen. Repeat with the rest of the flatbreads and keep warm.

Wipe out the pan and heat the remaining oil. Add the paprika and cook for 1 minute, until fragrant. Stir through the remaining yogurt.

Once the vegetables have cooked, slip the garlic out of their skins. Serve the vegetables on top of the yogurt with a drizzle of pomegranate molasses and a flatbread to dip.

Trout with Samphire and Mustard-dill Sauce

This light and sophisticated dish is simple and quick to prepare but impressive enough to make for guests. The dill and mustard sauce is a classic Scandinavian accompaniment; any leftovers can be used as a dressing for smoked salmon or shaved beetroot. Use any leftover dill in the Bean and Dill Pilaf with Green Tahini (see page 84).

SERVES: 4 | PREP TIME: 10 mins | COOKING TIME: 15–20 mins

750g (1lb 10oz) new
  potatoes
4 trout fillets, about
  125g (4oz) each
4 tbsp rapeseed
  or olive oil
90g (3½oz) samphire
1 lemon
A small bunch of dill
3 tbsp Dijon mustard
1 tbsp runny honey
1 tbsp cider vinegar
20g (¾oz) butter

Preheat the oven to 200°C / 180°C fan / gas mark 6.

Scrub the new potatoes. Halve any larger ones so that they are all roughly the same size. Put on to boil for 12–15 minutes, until just tender.

Place the trout fillets on a non-stick baking tray, drizzle with 1 tbsp of the oil and season. Bake for 10–12 minutes, until the flesh flakes easily to the touch.

Wash the samphire and remove any tough, woody ends. Cut the lemon into wedges. Finely chop the dill. Whisk together the mustard, honey, vinegar, dill and the remaining oil. Season and add lemon juice to taste.

Once the potatoes are just about tender, add the samphire and simmer for a final 30 seconds. Drain well and toss in the butter. Season with caution as the samphire is very salty.

Serve the trout, potatoes and samphire with the sauce spooned over or to the side so that everyone can help themselves.

Leek and Butter Bean Stew with Butter and Thyme Crumbs

A simple yet indulgent stew that can be adapted to suit any season. Cavolo nero is used in this wintry version but can be swapped for any seasonal green. Instead of being baked, the stew is topped with breadcrumbs and grilled until crisp and golden. Keep an eye on the breadcrumbs to avoid them catching. Use any remaining thyme in the Corn and Chorizo Chowder (see page 16).

SERVES: 4 | VEGETARIAN | PREP TIME: 10 mins | COOKING TIME: 30 mins

40g (1½oz) butter

30g (1¼oz) fresh
    breadcrumbs

4 sprigs of thyme,
    leaves stripped

2 tsps olive oil

1 shallot, peeled
    and finely sliced

1 rib of celery,
    trimmed and
    finely chopped

2 cloves of garlic

500g (1lb 2oz) leeks

2 x 400g (14oz) cans
    of butter beans

550ml (19fl oz)
    vegetable stock

200g (7oz) cavolo nero

1½ tbsp wholegrain
    mustard

60ml (4 tbsp) double
    cream

Melt the butter in a large sauté pan with a lid. Spoon off half and stir through the breadcrumbs and thyme. Season and set aside.

Add the oil to the pan and cook the shallots and celery for 4–5 mins, until just softened. Peel and crush the garlic. Trim and cut the leeks into 1cm (⅜in) thick rounds. Drain and rinse the beans in a sieve. Add the garlic and leeks to the pan, cook for 1 min, then pour in the stock, cover and simmer gently for 15 mins.

Meanwhile, strip the tough stalks from the cavolo nero and finely shred the leaves. Add to the stew with the mustard and cream and simmer for 2–3 mins, until just wilted.

Heat the grill to medium. Transfer the stew to an ovenproof dish and sprinkle over the breadcrumbs. Grill for 2–3 mins, until crisp and golden.

Pork Chops Agrodolce, Blistered Beans and Parmesan Butter Bean Mash

Agrodolce is a traditional Italian sweet-and-sour sauce, which in this recipe comprises raisins, red wine vinegar, a little sugar and pine nuts to cut through the richness of the pork chops. The cooking times are based on thick-cut pork chops, so adjust according to what you buy.

SERVES: 4 | PREP TIME: 10 mins | COOKING TIME: 25 mins

40g (1½oz) golden
   raisins or sultanas
½ a red onion
2 tbsp pine nuts
3 tbsp olive oil
200ml (7fl oz)
   chicken stock
2 x 400g (14oz) cans
   butter beans
4 thick pork chops
200g (7oz) fine
   green beans
50g (2oz) Parmesan
3 tbsp red wine
   vinegar
1½ tbsp sugar

Cover the raisins with 3 tbsp of boiling water and set aside to soak. Peel and slice the onion. Toast the pine nuts in a large, non-stick frying pan for 1–2 minutes, until golden. Remove from the pan and set aside.

Add 1 tbsp of the oil to the pan and gently fry the onion for 5 minutes, until beginning to soften. Remove and set aside. Heat the stock in a saucepan. Drain the butter beans, add to the saucepan and simmer gently for 8 minutes.

Pat the pork chops dry and season well. Heat another tbsp of oil in the frying pan. Add the chops and fry for 5 minutes each side, until browned. Meanwhile, trim the green beans. Finely grate the Parmesan. Mash the butter beans, stir through the cheese and season. Keep warm.

Lower the heat slightly and return the onion and pine nuts to the pan. Pour in the vinegar, sugar and the raisins with their soaking water. Continue to cook for a further 2–3 minutes, until just cooked through. Once the pork is cooked, remove from the pan and keep warm. Wipe out the pan and heat the remaining oil over a high heat. Add the green beans and fry for 2–3 minutes, until blistered. Serve alongside the pork and butter-bean mash.

Veggie Sausage and Kale Bake with Cheesy Polenta

Simple and family friendly, this recipe makes a great alternative to traditional sausages and mash. Choose firm vegetarian sausages to ensure that they can hold their shape when roasted. Polenta firms up quickly so make up just before serving; any leftovers can be set, sliced and baked into chips.

SERVES: 4 | PREP TIME: 5 mins | COOKING TIME: 25 mins

1 large red onion
4 sprigs of thyme
8 vegetarian sausages
1 tbsp olive oil
100g (3½oz) Cheddar cheese
1 tbsp wholegrain mustard
150ml (5fl oz) beef or chicken stock
200g (7oz) shredded kale
1 tbsp red onion chutney
150g (5oz) express polenta
A knob of butter

Preheat the oven to 200°C / 180°C fan / gas mark 6.

Peel, halve and cut the onion into slim wedges. Strip the leaves from the thyme. Tip the onion, thyme and sausages into a large roasting tin, pour over the oil and turn to coat. Spread out in a single layer and bake for 20 minutes.

Meanwhile, grate the cheese. Mix the mustard into the stock.

After 20 minutes, add the kale to the tin, turn the sausages and onion and pour over the mustard, chutney and stock. Bake for a further 5 minutes, until the sausages are golden and the kale is tender.

To prepare the polenta, pour 750ml (1½ pints) boiled water into a large saucepan and place over a high heat. Pour the polenta into the pan in a steady stream and stir continuously until the mixture is thickened and creamy. Stir in the cheese and butter and season to taste.

Serve the polenta topped with the sausage and kale bake.

Sausage, Lentil and Rosemary Stew

This short-cut stew provides comfort and flavour with minimal time at the stove. The key is to simmer the lentils separately to the sausages so that they can cook quickly while you prepare everything else. Passata with soffritto is available in most supermarkets and is a brilliant store-cupboard staple for adding flavour in double-quick time. The stew doesn't need much embellishment, but you can add some freshly chopped rosemary and a squeeze of lemon to freshen things up at the end, if you like.

SERVES: 4 | PREP TIME: 5 mins | COOKING TIME: 30–35 mins

150g (5oz) Puy lentils
750ml (1½ pints) hot chicken stock
2 sprigs of rosemary
1 tbsp olive oil
12 chipolatas or vegetarian alternative
1 echalion shallot
2 garlic cloves
150ml (5fl oz) red wine
400g (14oz) passata with soffritto
1 tbsp red pesto

Rinse the lentils in a sieve. Pour the hot stock into a large saucepan, add the lentils and one of the sprigs of rosemary and simmer for 15–20 minutes, until the lentils are just tender but with a little bite.

While the lentils are cooking, heat the oil in a large saucepan or flameproof casserole dish. Add the sausages and fry for 3–4 minutes, until lightly browned.

Peel, halve and finely slice the shallot. Peel and crush the garlic. Strip the needles from the remaining rosemary and finely chop. Add the shallot and chopped rosemary to the pan and cook gently for 4–5 minutes, until beginning to soften. Add the garlic, cook for 1 minute and then pour in the red wine. Bubble for 1 minute before adding the passata and red pesto. Simmer for 15 minutes, until the sausages are cooked through and tender.

Once the lentils are cooked, pour into the pan (with the stock) and simmer for a final 5 minutes, until the stew is slightly thickened and reduced. Check for seasoning, discard the rosemary sprig and serve ladled into bowls.

Desserts

Strawberry and Elderflower Fool

This summer dessert is lighter than air and can be prepared in 20 minutes. The fool will become firmer after a couple of hours in the fridge but for those with less time (or patience), you can enjoy a softer fool straight away. Serve with shortbread biscuits on the side or crumbled over the top.

SERVES: 4 | VEGETARIAN | EQUIPMENT: Electric whisk | PREP TIME: 20 mins, plus chilling

250g (9oz) strawberries
½ a lemon
200ml (7fl oz) double cream
100g (3½oz) Greek yogurt
3 tbsp elderflower cordial
Shortbread biscuits, to serve

Hull the strawberries. Roughly chop half and mash the remainder with a fork. Finely zest the lemon half.

Pour the cream, yogurt and cordial into a bowl and whisk until soft peaks form. Gently fold the crushed strawberries and lemon zest through the cream to create a slightly rippled effect.

Divide the chopped strawberries between glasses, saving a few for decoration. Spoon over the cream and top with the remaining chopped berries. Refrigerate for 2 hours before serving with the biscuits, if you can bear to wait.

Apricot and Pistachio Danish Pastry Tart

Buttery puff pastry is topped with thick custard and sunny apricots in this riff on a traditional Danish pastry. Enjoy as a dessert with extra custard or cream, or as a mid-morning treat with a coffee. The tart works best with the creamy custard found in the fresh aisle of the supermarket.

SERVES: 4 | VEGETARIAN | PREP TIME: 10–15 mins | COOKING TIME: 15–20 mins

320g (11oz) ready-rolled puff pastry sheet

1 large egg yolk

1 x 400g (14oz) can apricot halves

20g (¾oz) pistachios

150g (5oz) shop-bought vanilla custard

2 tbsp soft-set apricot jam

Preheat the oven to 220°C / 200°C fan / gas mark 7. Place a baking sheet on the top shelf of the oven.

Unroll the puff pastry sheet onto another baking sheet lined with parchment. Use a sharp knife to score a 1.5cm (½in) border around the edges, without cutting all the way through. Set aside in the fridge.

Whisk the egg yolk with a fork, until smooth. Drain the apricot halves. Reserve 1 tbsp of the syrup. Roughly chop the pistachios.

Remove the pastry from the fridge and brush the borders with a little of the egg yolk. Stir the remaining egg yolk through the custard and spread over the pastry, keeping within the borders. Arrange the apricots over the custard, cut-side down. Carefully slide the parchment onto the hot baking sheet and bake for 15–20 minutes, until well risen, crisp and golden.

Meanwhile, mix the jam with the reserved syrup. Once the tart is cooked, brush over the apricots and cut into slices to serve.

Pineapple Sorbet with Lime and Mint

Incredibly simple and refreshing, this sorbet, made with frozen pineapple, is ready in an instant. Popped in a food processor with some mint, lime, and maple syrup, the pineapple will turn light, smooth and airy within a few minutes. Serve straight away, store in the freezer or even serve with a little rum and soda to make a frozen cocktail.

SERVES: 4 | VEGAN | EQUIPMENT: Food processor | PREP TIME: 20 mins, plus freezing

1 medium, ripe pineapple

1 lime

3 sprigs of mint

2 tbsp maple syrup

Peel, core and finely chop the pineapple. Transfer to a freezer bag and freeze for at least 6 hours.

Finely zest half of the lime and roughly chop the mint. Tip the lime zest and mint into a food processor with the frozen pineapple and maple syrup and process until smooth and light. Serve immediately or freeze scoops into a punnet and freeze for later. Sit at room temperature for 10 minutes before serving.

Orange and Blueberry Friands

Friands are elegant little cakes, popular in Australia and New Zealand. Very light in texture with a crisp edge, they freeze well and will keep for 2–3 days after baking. When folding the dry ingredients into the egg whites, use a large metal spoon and stop as soon as the ingredients are incorporated to keep the cakes as airy as possible.

SERVES: 4 | **VEGETARIAN** | **EQUIPMENT:** Electric whisk | **PREP TIME:** 20 mins | **COOKING TIME:** 20 mins

100g (3½oz) butter, plus extra for greasing
1 unwaxed orange
4 medium egg whites
125g (4oz) icing sugar
75g (3oz) plain flour
A pinch of salt
85g (3¼oz) ground almonds
100g (3½oz) blueberries

Preheat the oven to 200°C / 180°C fan / gas mark 6.

Grease 8 holes of a non-stick friand or cupcake tin well with butter. Melt 100g (3½oz) of butter and set aside to cool. Finely grate the zest of the orange.

In a separate bowl, whisk the egg whites until they form very soft peaks. Sift the icing sugar, flour and a pinch of salt over the egg whites and sprinkle over the almonds and orange zest, breaking up any clumps as you go.

Pour over the butter and very gently fold everything together, until just combined. Divide between the prepared holes in the tin and add a few blueberries to each cake. Bake for 18–20 minutes, until risen, golden and just firm.

Peanut Butter French Toast

The addition of peanut butter to the custard mix for this French toast gives it a subtle nuttiness – delicious with a sweet and slightly tart blueberry compôte. The compôte will freeze well so make double for an even speedier dessert next time.

SERVES: 4 | VEGETARIAN | PREP TIME: 10 mins | COOKING TIME: 12–14 mins

200g (7oz) frozen
  blueberries
1 tbsp runny honey
2 large eggs
125g (4oz) smooth
  peanut butter
150ml (5fl oz)
  whole milk
1 tsp vanilla extract
4 thick slices
  of brioche
Butter, for frying
Icing sugar, to serve

Tip the blueberries into a pan with 1 tbsp water and the honey. Bring up to the boil and simmer gently for 6–8 minutes, until split and juicy.

Meanwhile, whisk together the eggs and peanut butter until fairly smooth. Gradually whisk in the milk, followed by the vanilla extract. Lay the brioche slices out in a dish and pour over the egg mixture. Leave to soak for 2 minutes, then turn over and soak for a further 2 minutes.

Melt the butter in a large frying pan. Carefully lift two of the brioche slices out of the pan and fry for 2–3 minutes each side, until crisp and golden. Keep warm and repeat with the other slices.

Serve with the blueberry compôte and a dusting of icing sugar.

Grilled Mango with Coconut and Lime Cream

This dessert is as simple to prepare as it gets but still completely delicious. The perfumed sweetness of the mango is wonderful with clouds of softly whipped coconut cream and a tangy hit of lime. Be sure to refrigerate the coconut cream well before whipping, otherwise it won't hold the air.

SERVES: 4 | VEGAN | EQUIPMENT: Electric whisk | PREP TIME: 15 mins | COOKING TIME: 4–5 mins

4 tbsp coconut chips
2 ripe mangoes
1½ tbsp vegetable or sunflower oil
1½ tbsp soft light brown sugar
1 lime
200ml (7fl oz) coconut cream, refrigerated for at least 2 hours
1½ tbsp icing sugar

Heat a griddle pan over a medium flame. Toast the coconut chips briefly, until golden; keep a close eye on them as they can catch and burn very quickly. Remove from the pan and set aside.

Cut the cheeks of the mangoes away from the stones. Mix the oil with the sugar and brush over the cut sides of the mangoes. Griddle for 2–3 minutes, until caramelised. Set aside to cool slightly.

Meanwhile, finely grate the lime zest. Cut the lime into wedges. Spoon the cream into a bowl and sift over the icing sugar. Beat with an electric whisk until soft and airy. Fold through the lime zest.

Let the mangoes cool a little before serving with a dollop of cream sprinkled with the coconut chips and a wedge of lime.

White Chocolate and Passion Fruit Pots

These little pots combine the sweet creaminess of white chocolate with the slightly sharp, fragrant flavour of passion fruit. White chocolate can be tricky to work with but this method will ensure a smooth, glossy ganache every time.

SERVES: 4 | **VEGETARIAN** | **PREP TIME:** 15 mins, plus setting | **COOKING TIME:** 2–3 mins

3 passion fruit
200g (7oz) white
   chocolate
250ml (9fl oz)
   double cream
2 large egg yolks
1 tbsp icing sugar

Cut open the passion fruit and push the pulp of two through a sieve. Reserve a few of the seeds for serving. Finely chop the chocolate and put in a heatproof bowl with the strained passion fruit.

Heat the cream until it is beginning to boil at the edges of the pan. Remove from the heat and pour over the chocolate and strained passionfruit. Leave to sit for 1 minute, then stir the cream into the chocolate, beginning in the centre and gradually moving outwards, until melted and smooth. Stir in the egg yolks, pour into a jug and divide between four small glasses.

Leave to set for at least 2 hours or overnight. When ready to serve, mix the remaining passion fruit with the icing sugar and spoon over the pots.

Hotcakes with Cinnamon and Honey Butter

Japanese-style hotcakes are fluffier and slightly sweeter than an American pancake, making them fit for a dessert or brunch. The honey and cinnamon butter is very easy and quick to prepare – the butter just needs to be soft and at room temperature. Keep the first batch of pancakes warm in a low oven while you're cooking the rest.

SERVES: 4 | VEGETARIAN | PREP TIME: 10 mins | COOKING TIME: 20 mins

40g (1½oz) soft butter
2 tbsp runny honey
1 tsp ground
   cinnamon
200g (7oz) self-raising
   flour
1 tsp baking powder
50g (2oz) caster sugar
A pinch of salt
2 large eggs
1½ tbsp sunflower or
   vegetable oil, plus
   extra for frying
200ml (7fl oz) milk
250g (9oz) berries,
   to serve

Put the butter, honey and cinnamon in a mixing bowl and whisk together until light and fluffy. Set aside for now.

Sift the flour and baking powder into a large mixing bowl. Stir through the sugar and a pinch of salt.

Make a well in the centre of the flour, crack in the eggs and add the oil. Use a whisk to beat the eggs and gradually whisk in the milk, drawing in the flour as you go.

Once the batter is smooth, heat a non-stick pan and wipe with a little oil. Add large tablespoons of the batter, cover with a lid and fry over a low heat for 2–3 minutes, until bubbles appear on the surface. Carefully flip over and cook for a further 1–2 minutes, until golden. Keep warm and repeat with the remaining batter.

Serve the hotcakes with the honey and cinnamon butter and berries.

Banoffee Puddings

These little sponge puddings will feed four generously; the mixture will fit four dariole moulds (like mini metal pudding basins) perfectly, but you might get up to six portions if using ramekins. Use a shop-bought caramel that is thick and spoonable. Serve with cream or vanilla ice cream – or both.

SERVES: 4 | VEGETARIAN | EQUIPMENT: Electric whisk | PREP TIME: 15 mins | COOKING TIME: 20–25 mins

125g (4oz) soft butter (plus extra for greasing)
1 medium banana
4 tbsp ready-made caramel (such as Carnation)
125g (4oz) light soft brown sugar
1 tsp vanilla extract
2 medium eggs
125g (4oz) self-raising flour
A pinch of salt
Cream or vanilla ice cream, to serve

Preheat the oven to 180°C / 160°C fan / gas mark 4.

Thoroughly grease four ramekins or dariole moulds with butter. Cut the banana into rounds 0.5cm (¼in) thick and lay a few slices in the base of each mould. Top each one with 1 tbsp of caramel and set aside.

Put the butter, sugar and vanilla extract in a mixing bowl and beat until light, pale and fluffy. Break in an egg, beat to combine and repeat with the remaining egg.

Sift over the flour, add a pinch of salt and gently fold through. Divide between the moulds (only fill to three-quarters), place on a baking tray and bake for 20–25 minutes, until well risen and a skewer inserted into the centre comes out clean.

The caramel will be ferociously hot, so leave to stand for a few minutes before running a knife around the edges of the puddings and turning out onto plates. Serve with cream or ice cream.

Roasted Vanilla Plums with Oat and Hazelnut Crumble

This autumnal dessert is perfect for cosy evenings when the nights are starting to draw in. The plums are roasted quickly so need to be ripe; they will be softened and slightly jammy but still retain their shape, unlike in a traditional crumble. The topping is quick to prepare and is cooked separately to the plums to ensure a crisp texture. Serve with cream, custard or ice cream, or even with Greek yogurt for a breakfast treat.

SERVES: 4 | VEGETARIAN | PREP TIME: 15 mins | COOKING TIME: 25 mins

6 ripe plums
1 vanilla pod
1 orange
50g (2oz) light brown soft sugar
60g (2½oz) plain flour
50g (2oz) butter
25g (1oz) jumbo rolled oats
20g (¾oz) hazelnuts
Cream, custard or ice cream, to serve

Preheat the oven to 200°C / 180°C fan / gas mark 6.

Halve and de-stone the plums. Split the vanilla pod in half and scrape out the seeds. Juice the orange.

Lay the plums, cut-side up, in a single layer on a baking dish. Drizzle over the orange juice, add 2 tbsp of water and pop the vanilla pod and seeds into the dish. Sprinkle over half the sugar and bake in the oven for 25 minutes, until the fruit is slightly softened and sticky.

Meanwhile, tip the flour into a bowl. Chop the butter into cubes and rub into the flour. Stir in the remaining sugar and the oats. Roughly chop the hazelnuts, stir through and sprinkle onto a baking tray. Bake for 15 minutes, until crisp and golden.

Serve the plums sprinkled with the crumble and a generous helping of cream, custard or ice cream.

Malted Milk Chocolate Affogato

This take on an affogato combines a sweet, malty ice cream with the gentle bitterness of dark chocolate. The chocolate is simply melted into hot milk with a pinch of salt to emulate the hit of espresso. The no-churn ice cream couldn't be easier to make but does require overnight freezing time.

SERVES: 4 | VEGETARIAN | EQUIPMENT: Electric whisk | PREP TIME: 20 mins, plus overnight freezing

80g (3¼ oz) malt powder (such as Horlicks)

½ a 400g (14oz) can of condensed milk

300ml (10½fl oz) double cream

200ml (7fl oz) whole milk

4 malted milk biscuits

50g (2oz) dark chocolate

A pinch of sea salt

To make the ice cream, whisk the malt powder, condensed milk and cream together in a large bowl, until soft peaks form. Stir and whisk again. Transfer to a freezer-proof container or loaf tin and freeze for at least 6 hours, or overnight.

When you're ready to serve, make the hot chocolate. Heat the milk in a pan until steaming and bubbling at the edges. Meanwhile, crush the biscuits in a zip-lock bag with a rolling pin. Finely chop the chocolate and put in a jug with a pinch of salt. Gradually whisk in the hot milk to melt the chocolate.

Spoon the ice cream into cups or small bowls. Pour over the hot chocolate to serve and sprinkle over the biscuit crumbs.

Marmalade Baked Pears with Vanilla Mascarpone

Sweet, autumnal pears are made sticky and citrussy when baked with marmalade and freshly squeezed orange juice. The pears should be ripe but not too soft so that they hold their shape when baked.

SERVES: 4 | VEGETARIAN | PREP TIME: 10 mins | COOKING TIME: 25–30 mins

100g (3½oz) marmalade

2 oranges

4 Conference pears

250g (9oz) mascarpone

1 tsp vanilla-bean paste

Preheat the oven to 190°C / 170°C fan / gas mark 5.

Spoon the marmalade into a bowl and loosen with a whisk or fork. Juice the oranges and gradually add to the marmalade, until combined.

Halve the pears lengthways and use a teaspoon or knife to cut out the cores. Place in a baking dish and pour over the marmalade mixture. Bake in the oven for 25–30 minutes, until softened and sticky.

Meanwhile, beat together the mascarpone and vanilla paste. Serve alongside the pears.

St Clement's Trifles

Trifles are the ultimate in quick, crowd-pleasing desserts. These mini orange and lemon versions can be served straight after preparing or left to set in the fridge for a couple of hours. The orange liqueur adds a delightful kick but can be substituted for extra clementine juice.

SERVES: 4 | VEGETARIAN | EQUIPMENT: Electric whisk | PREP TIME: 30 mins

½ a small Madeira cake (about 100g (3½oz) weight)

1 lemon

4 clementines or satsumas

2 tbsp Cointreau or other orange liqueur

200ml (7fl oz) double cream

2 tbsp icing sugar

400g (14oz) thick custard

4 tbsp lemon curd

4 crisp amaretti biscuits

50g (2oz) toasted flaked almonds

Trim the Madeira cake and cut into 1cm (⅜in) cubes. Divide between 4 glasses. Finely grate the zest of half the lemon and one of the clementines. Squeeze the juice of the clementine and pour over the cake, along with the Cointreau. Peel and slice the remaining clementines and place on top of the sponge layer.

Whip the cream with the icing sugar until it forms soft peaks. Fold through the clementine zest. Divide the custard between the glasses and dollop over the lemon curd. Sprinkle over the lemon zest. Crush the amaretti biscuits. Top the trifles with the cream and finish with flaked almonds and amaretti crumbs.

Eton Mess Yogurt Bark

Brilliantly simple and quick to prepare, this frozen yogurt bark is certain to be a massive hit with children. Remove from the freezer 5–10 minutes before serving to ensure easy cutting.

SERVES: 4 | VEGETARIAN | EQUIPMENT: Electric whisk |
PREP TIME: 20 mins, plus overnight freezing

300g (10½oz) berries such as strawberries, raspberries and blueberries
500g (1lb 2oz) Greek yogurt
200ml (7fl oz) double cream
1 tsp vanilla extract
2 tbsp icing sugar
4 shop-bought meringue nests

If using strawberries, hull them and cut into quarters. Line a baking tray with parchment.

Tip the yogurt, cream and vanilla into a large mixing bowl. Sift over the icing sugar and whisk to combine.

Spread the mixture out onto the parchment – it should be about 1cm (⅜in) thick. Crumble over the meringue and sprinkle over the berries in an even layer. Freeze for a minimum of 4 hours. Cut into shards to serve.

Index

Vegan and vegetarian recipes in **bold**

Acknowledgments

Thank you to all at Pavilion Books and the National Trust for entrusting me with this title; it has been a joy to work on.

Thank you to Peter Taylor for commissioning me and for steering the direction of the book. Thank you so much to Kristy Richardson for your brilliant editing, for including me in everything and for understanding the constraints of working around a small child! To Katie Hewett for your incredibly thorough copy editing and to Betsy Hosegood for your proofreading. To Gemma Doyle and Lynne Lanning, the design and layout of the book is wonderful thanks to your work. And to Verity Rimmer from the National Trust; thank you for your enthusiasm for my ideas.

A big thank you to the super talented Dan Jones, always ready with a dry quip and a killer playlist. The photography is beautiful and I feel really lucky that you shot this book. Thank you to Charlie Clapp for spinning the plates and pans and for making the food look delicious. Thank you to Kitty Coles for the wonderful props; they were perfect for enhancing the food and making it look relaxed.

A final thank you to my partner, Bob, and our son, Albie, for being my chief taste testers and my reason for loving to cook.